T0329383

# THE UNITED STATES

# THE UNITED STATES

## AN HISTORICAL SKETCH

BY

### E. A. BENIANS
*Master of St John's College*
*Cambridge*

CAMBRIDGE
AT THE UNIVERSITY PRESS
1943

# CAMBRIDGE
## UNIVERSITY PRESS

University Printing House, Cambridge CB2 8BS, United Kingdom

Published in the United States of America by Cambridge University Press, New York

Cambridge University Press is part of the University of Cambridge.

It furthers the University's mission by disseminating knowledge in the pursuit of
education, learning and research at the highest international levels of excellence.

www.cambridge.org
Information on this title: www.cambridge.org/9781107658844

© Cambridge University Press 1943

First published 1943
First paperback edition 2014

A catalogue record for this publication is available from the British Library

ISBN 978-1-107-65884-4 Paperback

# PREFACE

Four lectures given to a Cambridge audience with the object of showing something of the content and interest of American history have been somewhat expanded in the following historical sketch of the United States in the hope that in this form they may serve the same purpose in a wider field. The titles of the chapters indicate the sequence of American historical development which I have endeavoured to follow. 'The New Nation' surveys the course of events from the establishment of independence to the end of the Napoleonic Wars; 'Western Settlement' treats of westward expansion down to the Civil War and its influence on American life and institutions; 'The Union' deals with the origins and consequences of the great struggle to preserve the unity of the nation; 'Industrial Greatness' with the economic expansion of the country; and 'The New World and the Old' with the developments of the twentieth century. The American achievement is not the least significant chapter in the history of human freedom, and in days when the successful collaboration of Great Britain and the United States may do so much to determine whether that history shall become an ampler story or a tale that is told, there is an awakened desire for the mutual knowledge and understanding which is the firmest foundation of friendship. I hope that this sketch, slight as it is, may be of some use to those who have not the chance of reading more widely by making clear a few of the leading facts and principles in the history of the United States.

I am most grateful to my friends, Mr T. R. Glover and Mr M. P. Charlesworth, Fellows of my own College and fellow-students of things American, for reading the book in manuscript and for many invaluable suggestions.

E. A. B.

*November* 1942

# CONTENTS

# CONTENTS

# CHAPTER I

## The New Nation

'If there be one fact in the world perfectly clear it is this: "That the disposition of the people of America is wholly averse to any other than a free government."' EDMUND BURKE: *Letter to the Sheriffs of the City of Bristol on the Affairs of America* (1777)

The future greatness of the American Republic was early predicted. Adam Smith, in the *Wealth of Nations*, published in 1776, the year of the Declaration of Independence, foretold that the Americans would create 'an extensive empire', 'one of the greatest and most formidable that ever was in the world'. He saw them becoming richer than England in little more than a century. He would have welcomed American representatives in the British Parliament and formed of Great Britain and her colonies an Anglo-American empire of which the seat would in due course remove itself to the other side of the Atlantic.[1] This logic might come easy to a Scottish professor, but it did not accord with American ambition or English traditions. When, a generation later, Napoleon, selling Louisiana to the United States, prophesied her future greatness—'Whatever nation holds the valley of the Mississippi', he said, 'will eventually be the most powerful on earth'[2]—there was more to go upon.

By that time the United States had not only established her unity and the form of her institutions, but had begun the marvellous expansion of settlement into the Mississippi valley. Before the middle of the nineteenth century she had, in several strides of growth, assumed her present territorial form, and waves of settlement had rolled across the continent to the Pacific coast. That process proceeded with little interruption through the long

[1] *Wealth of Nations*, ed. Nicholson, J. S., pp. 257–8.
[2] Carpenter, E. J., *The American Advance*, p. 35.

struggle for unity which filled the third quarter of the century. The dividing forces were overcome by the forces of growth. The current of immigration from the Old World that poured un- ceasingly into the country, the spread of railways in all directions linking up the remotest parts of the continental area, the rise of giant industries supplying the needs of a vast market—these were processes of unification and strengthening which brought into being, before the end of the nineteenth century, what Adam Smith had predicted, 'an extensive empire', 'one of the greatest and most formidable that ever was in the world'.

As colonies and parts of a European state the Americans had been in the European system and their fortunes were bound up with what happened in Europe. But in their large and distant country they had built up a life and interests which they felt they could best manage themselves and best manage apart from Europe. The cities and states they had founded gave them confidence in their own powers; the result of the Seven Years' War gave them security; and they had come to perceive that in North America was a vast theatre for human affairs on which they could play a greater part as an independent nation than as an appendage to their mother country. British statesmen in 1763 knew that they faced a large problem of imperial reorganization, but they were on an uncharted ocean. Wise after the event, we can see that they had not sufficient knowledge of America, nor imagination enough, to produce a countervailing offer to this attractive prospect. If Grenville and his successors could have visualized an Anglo- American union on equal terms, they might not have seen the United States of America. But if British statesmanship failed at this crisis, English colonization was vindicated in its powerful and adventurous sons who drew the sword in defence of their own freedom and importance and established a new nation in a new world. That it was done by war necessarily gave a bias to the course of American history. The Declaration of Independence long reverberated in Anglo-American relations.

The great question when the War of Independence ended was

what would be the future of the American colonies. Victory gave them their freedom, but how would it be used? Would they form a strong American state or remain a group of small republics? Under the style of the United States of America they had agreed upon a union during the war (1781). But its bonds were very loose and its downfall was freely predicted. Its Parliament, the Continental Congress, had been granted many powers in the Articles of Confederation, but they were powers on paper, and it had little power in fact. Each State retained its sovereignty, freedom and independence and each went its own way in democratic reforms and economic experiment, while the aftermath of war—deranged currency, rising prices, unemployment, burdensome debt—lay upon the population. Congress did not lack men of ability, but, without money and without police, it could not keep peace and order at home or lift the country out of financial chaos, while, abroad, it was forfeiting all respect, because it could not pay the debts incurred in the war or enforce the terms of the peace. Economic disaster threatened the country when each State was free to regulate foreign trade and deal with currency problems according to its own ideas and interests. Experience, as Alexander Hamilton said, showed that the confederation was radically defective.

But if the Confederacy dissolved, what would take its place? John Adams had written sarcastically of the 'beauties and sublimities' of a Continental Congress, but if it disappeared from the scene, then even the semblance of unity and common government was gone. No protection remained to the States against foreign danger or even against the spectre some saw on the horizon—of restored monarchy. This was a situation to test the soundness of the political instinct and experience of the Americans. For five years, 1783–8, the future remained in doubt, and these years have been called the critical period in American history. Discontent bred disorder and even a rebellion in Massachusetts, which excited widespread alarm. 'There are combustibles in every state, which a spark might set fire to', wrote

Washington. Substantial men, landowners and merchants, began to tremble for the interests of property. But if democrats and debtors sought to reap the fruits of the American Revolution, there were also conservatives and creditors ready to strengthen government and enforce law. Out of the confusion there came, so writes an American historian,[1] 'an emotional surge, without which nothing great can be accomplished in America—towards a new federal constitution'.

The turning-point was a dispute between Virginia and Maryland, concerning the navigation of the Potomac, which led on to a conference of several States. Those leading men who wished something done to save the nation took advantage of the prevailing anxiety and proposed a general convention to revise the form of government and make it adequate to the country's needs. The State legislatures rose to the occasion, appointed delegates, and, in the summer of 1787, the historic convention which devised the constitution of the United States assembled in the State House at Philadelphia. The delegates gathered in a mood of doubt and hesitation. Would the people accept the stronger government which the situation demanded? Was it practical politics to propose an effective plan? Tradition preserves the picture of Washington, 'standing self-collected' in the midst of the doubters. If, to please the people, he said, we offer what we ourselves disapprove, how can we afterwards defend our work? Let us raise a standard to which the wise and honest can repair.

Unlike another assembly, more famous in history but less fortunate in its work, which opened its sessions at Versailles two years later, the Philadelphia convention was a small body. Sixty-two delegates were appointed by the States, fifty-five attended and in the end thirty-nine signed the constitution. Solid interests were better represented amongst them than idealist theory, but what was best represented was the political experience of America and its capacity for self-government. Most of the members were leading men in their States—landowners, merchants, lawyers—

[1] Morison, S. E., *History of the United States*, I, 81.

most of them knew the working of the Parliamentary system, and most of them were under forty years old. For so youthful a body their outlook was realistic and rather conservative, equally nervous of extreme democracy and of a revived tyranny. 'Experience must be our only guide', said John Dickinson of Delaware, 'Reason may mislead us.' At Versailles the French orators, overflowing with idealism, declaimed before the public, and the galleries influenced the final vote; the American delegates sat in secret—indeed, not until 1840 were their proceedings published—so men could speak with freedom and heat and afterwards retract, and long debates and stormy struggles could end in compromise and mutual concession. But there were no reactionaries amongst them, no bitter heritage of social hatred, nor the urgent foreign danger which disturbed the course of the French Revolution. Some of them were not unconscious that more than their own fortune was at stake and that they stood at the bar of history. 'We are digesting a plan', said Madison, 'which may decide for ever the fate of republican government.'[1]

The success of the Convention was a result not only of the political wisdom of a remarkable group of men, but also of conditions of high importance which favoured American unity, particularly the geographical proximity of the thirteen colonies and their substantial unity of race and political tradition. Equally the problems about which they debated so arduously arose out of the history and rivalries of the colonies and the diversity of their circumstances. To their new life they brought a rich inheritance from their colonial days, but, with the potentialities of a great State, they inherited also the strongest local attachments and some mutual distrust.

The colonies had all been planted on the Atlantic coast belt of the continent, of which they had acquired continuous possession, and it was this contiguity which made their union possible. English efforts to unite them in colonial days for defence against

[1] *Documents illustrative of the formation of the Union of the American States*, selected, arranged and indexed by C. C. Tansill, p. 281.

the Indians and the French in Canada had all failed. Apart from
the geographical difficulties in the way of union and the strength
of local feeling, the colonies knew that union would bring stronger
government and they would not have that at English hands.
Only when they thought their liberty threatened did they overcome their separatist instinct. To a Congress which assembled
to resist the Stamp Act (1765) one of the delegates said: 'There
ought to be no New England man, no New Yorker, known on
this continent, but all of us Americans.' They had achieved
enough unity to win their independence, but would the new-
born American sentiment survive when danger had passed?

Local feeling was strengthened by differences of social and
economic life, which created a diversity of interests and outlook
between the States. Speaking generally, the population was
English and spoke English. Foreigners, French, Swedes, Dutch
and Germans, formed about one-fifth of the total of 4,000,000,
and they were chiefly in the Middle States. The negroes, numbering about 700,000, were for the most part in the South. In all
the States the middle-class yeomen of England made up the bulk
of the settlers and probably nowhere in the world was wealth
more evenly distributed. But in religious, social and economic
life there were important differences. The Anglican Church was
strong only in the South; in New England the various Puritan
bodies predominated and Maryland was partly Catholic. The
South, too, was a country of large plantations, worked by slaves,
with tobacco as the chief crop and even an accepted form of
currency. Agriculture was careless, and the South imported not
only manufactures but food. In the North agriculture was diversified, holdings were small, and slaves were a household luxury,
not used for field labour; foreign trade, fishing and shipbuilding
were important, and there were busy ports. Over the whole
country life was rural; not 3 per cent of the population were in
towns of 10,000 or over. New England reproduced the decorum
of English middle-class life; Southern society lived with more
style and ceremony. New England, with its common schools

and with Harvard College, founded in 1636 chiefly to train ministers, gave America the idea of an educated people; but the South, with Virginia at its head, was dominant in political and social life. Yale and other colleges were founded in the eighteenth century, but, throughout the colonial period, from Virginia and South Carolina, and to a less extent from Massachusetts, boys were sent to English schools, and young men to Oxford and Cambridge and the Inns of Court, to train for careers in Great Britain or America.[1] Massachusetts, Pennsylvania and Virginia were the three largest States, but there was no such supremacy of any one State or group as to prove a fatal bar to union. Moreover, their political institutions were much the same. All had enjoyed self-government and were familiar with the same political methods, and the same spirit of liberty prevailed in them all. In the South power was in the hands of the big planters and slaveowners, in the Middle Colonies of merchants and planters, while in New England a religious aristocracy of small farmers and ministers laid the foundations of local self-government.

With their traditions and experience, it is not surprising that in the eighteenth century the colonial assemblies had begun to feel themselves sovereign bodies, and it was the strength of this feeling, justified by independence and quickened by democratic changes, which presented the most formidable problem to the American leaders gathered at Philadelphia. Could local sovereignty and national unity subsist together? A strong authority was necessary, but there was dread of setting up a new tyranny. The Americans still, to use the phrase of Burke, snuffed the approach of tyranny in every tainted breeze. The liberty they had won from the British Parliament and Crown they were not going to lose to another government, even American.

To solve this fundamental problem the Convention proposed a federal form of State. The existing State Governments would be preserved, but would surrender certain specified powers to a

[1] Connely, Willard, 'Colonial Americans in Oxford and Cambridge' in *The American Oxonian*, January 1942.

national authority. Within its own sphere, thus limited and defined, this new authority was to have coercive power. This was the essence of the matter and the secret of the success of the constitution. A real government was created. Its powers were to include all those possessed by the Confederation, covering such matters as war and foreign relations, posts, coinage and the Western territory, and, in addition, a taxing power, power over the militia, naturalization, copyright, power to establish postroads and the regulation of foreign and inter-state commerce. By thus naming and limiting the powers of the federal government, they hoped to protect State and individual freedom from over-great strength and arbitrary action on its part.

This plan to restrict the powers of the federal government introduces one of the great questions of American history. The powers of the federal government have steadily grown. They have been extended to meet the growing needs of the nation. But from the beginning Americans divided on this issue—on one side, those who wished to strengthen and increase the national powers, on the other, those who wished to interpret strictly the words of the Constitution.

Powers not specifically delegated by the Constitution to the United States, nor prohibited by it to the States, were reserved to the States respectively or to the people. Thus in many important spheres the States were left in control, but it may be noted that they were prohibited from levying duties on imports or exports and the territory of the United States thus became a vast area of free trade, open to the enterprise of the nation, a fact of immense importance in its future economic expansion.

In form the federal government was to be in three branches:

(i) The executive, which, after much discussion, was vested in a single person, a President of the United States, who, in order to ensure the choice of the best man, was to be chosen by a special body of electors, appointed by the States. He was to be endowed with ample powers and was to hold office for four years. Nothing was specified about re-election.

(ii) The legislative, a Congress of the United States, which was to consist of two Houses, a House of Representatives, elected by the people, and a Senate, elected by the legislatures of the States;

(iii) The judicial, at the head of which was a Supreme Court, which should interpret the Constitution and prevent any organ of it from exceeding its powers.

The division of the Government into three separate branches, each with defined powers, and so organized as to act as a check on each other was intended to be a further security of liberty and to put a brake on hasty action.

In order to prevent the large States from tyrannizing over the small, it was provided that each State should have an equal vote, viz. two members, in the Senate, and to prevent the small from combining their forces against the large, in the House of Representatives representation was to be in proportion to population. It is an interesting fact that though the United States has been divided sectionally, East against West, and North against South, it has never been divided, large States against small. Yet this was the issue which, after prolonged debates, most nearly brought the Convention to deadlock. Benjamin Franklin, whose international fame and whose age of eighty-two entitled him to be the moral Mentor of the Convention, had to warn the delegates that they were sent to consult and not to contend, and when, after many vain days of debate, agreement seemed impossible, he rose and said: 'Neither ancient nor modern history can give us light....I move that we have prayers every morning.'[1] Later deliberations produced the great compromise of the Constitution—that each State should have an equal vote in the Senate.

The slaves offered a difficult problem to the framers of a popular government and particularly as their numbers and position differed so much in North and South. Slavery was a heritage of colonial days. From 1670 onwards the encouragement of the slave trade had been an important object of English policy, and

[1] *Documents*..., pp. 295, 822.

some of the American colonies, faced, like most new countries, with a scarcity of labour, had welcomed the regular supply the trade ensured. So slavery had taken root and spread wherever climate and soil favoured the cultivation of the great staple crops. Most Americans wanted slavery and the slave trade to come to an end. The law of England did not recognize slavery, and in England the abolition of the trade was already under discussion. But the Southerners wanted the slaves for their plantations and New England shipowners carried them. Madison and others 'thought it wrong to admit in the Constitution the idea that there could be property in men'.[1] But South Carolina and Georgia had to be conciliated and it was a question of union with slavery or no union at all. So the institution was recognized, though the word was not used. In the Constitution slaves are referred to as 'other persons', or 'persons held to service', or 'such persons as any of the States now existing shall think proper to admit'. And a compromise was reached on the problems they raised. The slave trade was not to be prohibited prior to 1808; the various States were left free to abolish or retain slavery as each thought fit; and in the enumeration of the population for the purpose of determining taxation and representation in Congress, a State was to include three-fifths only of its slaves. In making this compromise on slavery the Convention may well have thought that time would simplify, if it did not solve, this problem.

In their handling of this question the Convention laid up trouble for the future, but they deserved well of their country for their wise and bold solution of another great constitutional issue. Were the original States to secure for themselves a position of advantage in the Union, or to admit new States on a footing of equality? All the Western lands were placed at the disposal of Congress and it was provided that new States should be admitted on equal terms. Thus the plan was laid for the greatest and most successful colonization of modern history—the spread of the Americans from their Atlantic base over the valley of the

[1] *Documents...*, p. 618.

Mississippi. This was the law of American growth and it prevented a breach between the original States and their spreading settlements, between East and West in the country. It not only encouraged the occupation of the West, but it made the greatness of the United States.

This decision was hardly less important in its influence on American history than the Declaration of Independence. Equality of status and a proper attention to their affairs are essential conditions of good relations between mother country and growing colony. No European state had solved this problem in the eighteenth century. None could escape from the idea that colonies existed to serve the interests of the homeland, and thus none proved capable of creating an imperial system as attractive to their colonies as national independence. With the exception of philosophers like Adam Smith, few people in England could conceive of an empire in which England and America were joined in equal union. Thus it was only a question of time for all the colonial empires of the European states to collapse, the English first. The Americans were certainly fortunate in having their problem simplified by the proximity of their colonies, but they deserve credit for having learned the lesson of their own history. They took the risk that power would pass from the Atlantic seaboard to the Mississippi valley, and it did. But they have been richly rewarded in the result—the thirteen States have grown to forty-eight under the same Government.

One question the Convention left obscure: was the union indissoluble? The States were free to ratify or not to ratify the Constitution, but, if they ratified it, could they afterwards withdraw? The Articles of Confederation spoke of a 'perpetual union', but they reserved the sovereignty and independence of each State. The Constitution ordained 'a more perfect union' and restricted the sovereignty of the States. But it provided a procedure of amendment, excepting, however, the great compromise which guarded State rights, the equal vote in the Senate. To protect the weaker members the Senate was given its commanding position, which is one of the special features of the Constitution.

In September 1787 the work was complete, but some members still had their doubts, and not even Franklin's plea,[1] that 'every member of the Convention who may still have objections to it, would with me, on this occasion doubt a little of his own infallibility, and to make manifest our unanimity, put his name to this instrument', prevailed with all. While the last signatures were being appended Franklin, 'looking towards the President's chair, at the back of which a rising sun happened to be painted, observed...I have...often and often in the course of the Session, and the vicissitudes of my hopes and fears as to its issue, looked at that [sun] behind the President without being able to tell whether it was rising or setting; but now at length I have the happiness to know that it is a rising and not a setting sun.'[2]

Franklin spoke truly. The unity they had achieved was of greater significance even than independence. The growth of America must soon have made it impossible for Great Britain to coerce her colonies and the fruit plucked in 1776 would in any case have fallen. On the plane of universal history the Declaration of Independence had a far-reaching meaning in the extension of freedom. But for their own future their union mattered more. For if the States had fallen apart, they could never have attained economic and political greatness; they would have been involved in continual friction with each other; they might even in part have passed again under the dominion of some European power; for none regarded them at the time with friendly eyes, and Britain, France and Spain still thought of expansion of their possessions in America. When the Spanish colonies freed themselves from the mother land, they formed a number of States and have so remained; in nothing did the English colonies show a profounder political instinct than when they surrendered State independence to form the strong Government under which they have worked out their history. The Constitution thus sealed the work of the

[1] *Documents...*, p. 740.          [2] *Documents...*, p. 745.

Declaration of Independence; for 'life, liberty and the pursuit of happiness' could only be secured by unity. The impartial reader of their debates will admire so magnificent, wide-ranging and practical a discussion of the great problems of government, but most of all must he admire that men who differed so much had the wisdom to agree upon union and save North America from the divisions of Europe.

Though the Constitution begins: 'We, the people of the United States, do ordain and establish this Constitution...', the Convention did not propose to submit it to a popular vote, but to State Conventions elected for the purpose, and on its ratification by nine States, it was to take effect. On a popular vote it might have been rejected, for its framers, as we have seen, were not for the most part democrats, and popular feeling could easily have been excited against some of its provisions.

In a covering letter transmitting the Constitution, with this recommendation, to the President of the Continental Congress, Washington explained the spirit in which the Convention had made its decisions. 'It is obviously impracticable',[1] he wrote, 'in the federal government of these States, to secure all rights of independent sovereignty to each, and yet provide for the interest and safety of all: Individuals entering into society, must give up a share of liberty to preserve the rest.' 'In all our deliberations', he continued, 'we kept steadily in view the consolidation of our Union, in which is involved our prosperity, felicity, safety, perhaps our national existence.' Each State therefore had sacrificed 'points of inferior magnitude' for the general good and the proposals were the result of this spirit of amity and of mutual deference and concession.

The Constitution was now submitted to Conventions in the several States, and for a few months the issue still remained in doubt. One by one the State Conventions under the influence of their leaders adopted it, though in some of the largest States, Massachusetts, Virginia and New York, only by a narrow

[1] *Documents...*, p. 1003.

majority. By June 1788 the necessary nine assenting States had
been won.

The new constitution came into operation in March 1789.
At that moment it was only a scrap of paper. Would it work,
or would it prove to have some fatal flaw? Were federal and
republican government possible on so vast a scale? John Adams
did not expect it to be 'very stable or very firm'. 'It will prevent
us for a time from drawing our swords upon each other.'[1] None
could foresee its well-poised balance, its adaptability to circumstances, its power to win loyalty. Its builders had built better than
they knew.

It was a favouring circumstance that Washington was persuaded to stand for the Presidency and was unanimously elected,
the only President so elected. He knew his fellow countrymen;
his cool and steady temper inspired confidence and respect; he
could rise above popularity, and in a crisis show that he meant
to govern. His character was a great asset to the Americans at a
crucial moment. It fell to him and the able men he gathered
round him to bring into being the organs of government, to
resolve the first problems of domestic and foreign policy and to
create precedents in form and ceremony for a republican state.

He saw before him 'an ocean of difficulties'. 'Integrity and
firmness are all I can promise', he wrote; the result of the venture,
'Heaven alone can foretell'.[2] A soldier rather than a politician,
he disapproved of parties and chose for his heads of departments
and advisers men of different views who formed a kind of
Cabinet.

Which way things would go depended not only on popular
confidence in Washington, but also on a right solution of the
great problems that confronted the country and particularly
finance and foreign policy. Washington appointed Alexander
Hamilton Secretary of the Treasury and Thomas Jefferson to the
Department of State—the Foreign Office. The character of
Washington, the genius of Hamilton and the idealism of Jefferson

[1] Morison, I, 102 f.n.                    [2] Morison, I, 99.

determined the course of events. Hamilton believed in a govern-
ing class, as in Great Britain, whose constitution he admired, and
he thought that the Government should win the confidence of
the capitalist and business sections of the community by attention
to their interests. By attaching to itself the rich and the influential
it would be made strong enough for its work. 'We must take man
as we find him', he had said in the Convention, 'and not rely
on pure patriotism.' An opposite view was maintained by
Jefferson, who wanted America to be as unlike Europe as possible—a nation of farmers and not of capitalists. He thought
always in terms of liberty, believed in the people and wished to
prevent the concentration of power, with its danger of a new
tyranny. Hamilton from the North and Jefferson from the South
represented also the two great economic interests that were
brought together in the Union and were to contend for power
in it—the agricultural interest of the South and the mercantile,
financial and shipping interests of the North. Virginia was the
focus of the one, New York and Massachusetts of the other.
Abroad, the one looked to Great Britain and the other to France.
The course of events gradually brought into distinctness and into
opposition the two points of view. Domestic issues arose first and
were complicated before long by events in Europe.

Hamilton soon produced his proposals for dealing with the
financial questions—the debt, the revenue and the currency. In
the first place he set out to ensure the public credit of the Union.
America's credit would depend on how she dealt with her debts,
particularly the war debt of the various States and the Confederacy, and he laid down the principle of strict financial
honesty—the United States would redeem all its debts at their
face value, though some of its credit obligations had depreciated.
He proposed that the debts of the States should be taken over by
the Union as a national debt, which would attach creditors to
the Union and also give the States an interest in its credit and
prestige. Virginia and Maryland, whose debts were small, were
inclined to disagree. At a dinner party in Jefferson's house a deal

was made. It was agreed that the new capital of the United States should be located on the Potomac, between Virginia and Maryland, and not, as might have been arranged, in the more central Pennsylvania, and Jefferson, in return, supported the assumption of the State debts. Thus the capital was fixed in its present somewhat insalubrious situation.

Direct taxation is unpopular in new countries and from the beginning the United States looked chiefly to import duties for its revenue. The first attempt to fix a tariff showed the diverse interests of the various sections. The Southern States inclined to free trade because they imported practically everything, food and manufactures; the Middle States produced agricultural staples and wanted to protect them, while in New England, where the infant industries were born, the powerful shipping interest favoured freedom of trade. Hamilton wished to use the power to levy customs duties in such a way as to protect and encourage American trade and industry, but his famous Report on Manufactures (1792) had little immediate effect on policy.

Hamilton's Excise Act of 1791 included an excise on whisky. The frontiersmen claimed that whisky was a necessity of life and ought not to be taxed. They talked of resisting the federal officers. The Constitution gave the Government coercive power. Would Washington use it? He called out the militia and the rebels gave way. The so-called whisky rebellion of 1794 was a little incident, but of large significance. It showed that there was now a real national government and that individuals could not resist it. Henceforward resistance to the federal authority, if it came, must come along the line of defending State rights.

To provide the Government with an agent to manage its loans and collect its revenue, Hamilton recommended that a national bank should be chartered on the model of the Bank of England, with power to issue notes, which would thus furnish a uniform paper currency. This question raised a far-reaching controversy. Jefferson argued that the proposal was unconstitutional; banking was a matter for the States—it was not included in the powers given to the federal government. Hamilton's reply was that the Constitution empowered the Government to collect taxes and pay the debt and this power implied a power to charter a bank to be employed in these purposes. This was the famous doctrine of implied powers which came thus early on the scene and was to be the great instrument in extending the functions of the national authority.

Hamilton's opponents also regarded the national bank as a piece of class legislation, that would create a moneyed interest at the service of the federal government and strengthen the capitalistic interests of the North. The South and West favoured the State banks and suspected a system under the control of Northern capitalists. The battle once joined against a strongly controlled banking system was to continue all through American history.

Hamilton's measures thus brought into relief the different interests of the States and the different points of view or tendencies in political opinion from which the first political parties sprang. He strengthened the national government by winning for it credit at home and abroad and arming it with effective financial power. Henceforward it could hold the Union together and provide for the needs of the nation. But his policy did not consolidate the Union, for, while he attached some classes and interests, he alienated others. Jefferson felt that Hamilton, in funding the State debts, chartering a national bank and imposing a tariff, was using measures which would impair republican government, assimilate America to Europe and even make the federal government an engine of tyranny. He wanted to keep the national authority within its sphere and to insist on a strict construction of the Constitution. In 1793 he left Washington's Cabinet and formed a group of Republicans in opposition to the administration party who were called Federalists. So the party system began.

Meanwhile the course of foreign affairs exercised a powerful influence on the development of opinion. Democrats sympathized with the French Revolution and formed a political group who joined Jefferson's Republicans, thus creating the Democratic-Republican party. In the years 1793–5 parties were crystallizing on these issues of foreign and domestic policy. The Republicans believed that American republicanism was bound up with the victory of France, the Federalists that American unity and social order depended on the preservation of Britain. The struggle in Europe raised problems of the first magnitude for America and it thus fell to the first generation of American statesmen to make decisions of crucial importance to their country, determining its position in international politics. History gives prominence to their long contention for neutral rights, but the more important results of their policy are seen in their separation of American interests from those of Europe and in the political and territorial changes in the New World consequent on the European war.

The first question was, would the new American nation continue to take a place as of old in the European system of policy? And if it did, would it align itself with Great Britain for the sake of economic interest and social security, or with France on the ground of the alliance of 1778, still subsisting, and of political sympathies? The Federalists in power inclined to Great Britain, but relations with her since the Peace had been far from cordial. At the Peace the British Government had displayed a genuine intention to secure the friendship of America. The large concessions of Western territory and the access to the British North American fisheries which the Peace granted were in proportion to the magnitude of this object. British ministers had sought to avoid harsh discussions and to lay the foundations of future amity. Policy as well as sentiment pointed to the wisdom of friendship with the United States. But to end a civil war so that it leaves no wounds is a problem to tax the resources of statesmanship. The Peace made a good beginning, but it did not give the Americans what they greatly desired—a close commercial treaty with Great Britain; for their trade with Great Britain and the British West Indies was vital to their prosperity, and with independence they had lost the advantages as well as the restraints of the Navigation Acts. To modify our commercial system in the interests of the Americans required some sacrifice and so some wisdom and imagination, and while the matter hung fire, the treaty soon provided occasions of dispute. Great Britain was aggrieved by the treatment of the Loyalists—that large section of the colonial population which had taken the British side in the struggle. Driven from their homes during the war, many had already gone to plant British colonies in Nova Scotia and the valley of the St Lawrence, and others, by the action of the State legislatures, were now compelled to leave. Anxious to keep her hold over the fur trade and the interior, Great Britain retaliated for their sufferings at the hands of their exhausted and embittered countrymen by not handing over the frontier posts of the ceded territory, as she had engaged to do in the treaty, and by ignoring the commercial proposals of the Americans. So, with continual friction, matters dragged on for a decade, then the outbreak of war with France raised serious questions of neutral rights and showed American sympathy strongly on the side of France.

Washington earnestly desired peace. Another war would shatter the foundations of the Government. Advised by Hamilton, he believed peace at the time indispensable to the preservation of the American nation. 'If this country', he wrote in 1795, 'is preserved in tranquillity twenty years longer, it may bid defiance in a just cause to any power whatever; such in that time will be its population, wealth and resources.' His general view of American policy, as expressed later in his Farewell address, was that America should not implicate herself in the ordinary vicissitudes of European politics, which, owing to the distance of America from Europe, were not her concern. ''Tis our true policy', he said, 'to steer clear of permanent alliances with any portion of the foreign world...we may safely trust to temporary alliances for extraordinary emergencies.'[1] His object was to bring America out of her subordination to European policy and the

[1] Morison, I, 175, 202.

associations of her colonial days and to place her on the road of her own interests and concerns. He did not exclude a temporary alliance for a special purpose. The advantage of that was written too clearly in the history of the War of Independence for General Washington to forget it.

It was not easy to maintain this policy in the state of feeling then existing in America. But Washington stood firm for peace and neutrality in the European struggle and in 1794 sent over Chief Justice Jay to find a peaceful way out of Anglo-American difficulties. The concessions offered by Great Britain were not considerable. As she relied on her trade war in the struggle with France, she would not give way in essentials to the claims of neutrals, but she agreed at last to surrender the Western posts, and a method of settling other matters in controversy by joint commissions was arranged. Jay's treaty was very unpopular in America, where British diplomacy acquired more credit than it usually receives in England; but the Senate accepted it, though Washington complained that he was abused in terms that could scarcely be applied to a Nero. Opposition to and criticism of him had increased; 'curse on his virtues', wrote Jefferson to Madison in 1796, 'they've undone the country'.[1]

The treaty removed the immediate danger of an Anglo-American war and cleared away the diplomatic debris left by the Peace of 1783, but it was a poor substitute for that generous arrangement between the two nations for which leading men on both sides had hoped and which might have laid a basis of friendship between the two nations on whom the burden of maintaining human freedom was to rest. The difficulties that caused the failure are apparent, but they were not insuperable to men who saw that the object was worth the price. 'Magnanimity in politics', said Burke, 'is not seldom the truest wisdom.' This high virtue in these years neither nation attained and both were to find the truth in Burke's epigram. Britain, with far-reaching consequences, missed her opportunity of American friendship; America lost

[1] Channing, E., *History of the United States*, IV, 174-5.

her Loyalist sons, who carried their talent and traditions to the upbuilding of Canada.

Washington had set the course of the ship of state and that course was to be maintained. New pilots took the helm, but not to steer in the wake of a European power. The Revolutionary wars in Europe became the Napoleonic wars and brought America the old troubles on the ocean, but new opportunities on the continent. Before that change took place the Federalist party had fallen from power.

In 1800 American democracy asserted itself for the first time and Jefferson was elected President. The Southerners, supported by the growing West, defeated the merchants and shipowners of the Middle and Northern States. To Jefferson, monarchy, militarism and aristocracy were alike hateful; he proposed to apply the spirit of democracy to the problems of America and check the centralizing tendencies of the national authority—in foreign policy, to differentiate and separate America from Europe and, at home, to institute 'a wise and frugal government'. And his idealism was combined with considerable administrative capacity. He restored simplicity. The coach and four and the scarlet liveries, in which Washington delighted, were seen no more. Mr Jefferson, and not the President of the United States, was 'At Home' to his guests. Expenditure was checked; the door of hospitality was opened again to the foreign immigrant, and freedom of speech, which the Federalists had restricted, was reasserted. But the work which the Federalists had done was not undone. They had pulled things together after the Revolution and attached stable elements to the new order. They had made the Constitution function, had laid down the lines of American government and solved the first problems of a national existence. The knot of union was firmly tied and no one wished it untied. 'We are all Republicans; we are all Federalists', said Jefferson in his first Inaugural and set the seal on the achievements of his predecessors. The new party was to have almost sixty years of uninterrupted power, but the nation did not retrace its first steps. Facts were too much for theories. The federal government needed to be strong in order to provide for the growth of the country. Western democrats, as they became property owners, favoured security of property and the encouragement of capital. When they applied their ideas in political life, it was not to weaken government, but to get the control of it out of the hands of Eastern leaders into their own. So the first change of political parties was a change rather of men than of policies, and the new party took over the policy of its predecessors so completely, that in a few years the Federalists disappeared and for a brief period the strife of parties ended in an 'era of good feelings'.

At the turn of the century the prospect in Europe was changing. Peace came for a brief interval, and with it new problems and new opportunities for America. Washington, refusing a third term as President, retired thankfully to his Virginian farm, and Adams, his successor (1797), ended the French alliance and slipped out of the French noose, at the price of giving up American claims against France for her spoliation of American trade. Jefferson, at his entry upon office in 1801, reaffirmed America's policy— 'peace, commerce and honest friendship with all nations, entangling alliances with none...'. Then the sky clouded.

For some time France had been scheming to recover her colonial power in North America and in 1800 Napoleon obtained from Spain the retrocession of the old French colony of Louisiana. 'The day that France takes possession of New Orleans...', wrote Jefferson when he heard of it, 'we must marry ourselves to the British fleet and nation.' The navigation of the Mississippi and the use of the port of New Orleans was vital to the American West. Dealing with Spain about it had been difficult; it would be far more difficult to deal with France. Napoleon might revive the old danger to America from French colonial ambition, throw her into the arms of England and bind up her affairs again with the vicissitudes of European policy.

The cloud passed as speedily as it had gathered. In April 1803 Napoleon renewed the war with England and in the same month

offered to sell Louisiana to the United States. He would give
Great Britain a rival not an ally. In a state of war money would
be more useful to France than Louisiana, and Louisiana would
be more valuable to France in American than in French hands.
The bargain was promptly concluded and American territory
was extended to the Rocky Mountains. Jefferson, the strict con-
structionist, carried the transaction through. His doubts concerning the legality of the action he kept to himself and President
and Senate set the national interest above the constitutional issue.
By dropping the French alliance and purchasing Louisiana, the
United States gave new effect to Washington's policy—releasing
itself from its European connections, its attachment to France and
its possible dependence on England. What was more, the acquisition of Louisiana gave to the country its continental form—the
inward, westward, landward direction of its interests and its
prospect of world power.

In the life-and-death struggle that now engaged Europe the
behaviour of neutrals and belligerents became ever more in-
tolerable to each other. The British practice of impressing
seamen caused incidents offensive to the principles and the self-
respect of the young republic, while France and Britain between
them squeezed neutral trade out of existence. As a retaliation on
the combatants Jefferson tried the experiment of a complete
prohibition of trade, but that proved more damaging to America
than to them. The toughness which saved Britain from Napoleon
endangered her relations with the United States. But who are
we to criticize the men of 1811, who, with Europe ranged
against them, must either surrender a powerful weapon or face
another foe? With a population and revenue more than double
what they had been in 1790, with a large mercantile marine
and an effective government, America felt strong enough to
protect her interests and her dignity. Intervention in the European
war was not generally desired, and particularly not by New
England and the Middle States. But there was no reserve of
good-will to ease the strain of antagonistic policies and exasperat-

ing incidents. In the end the militant spirit of the West, which thought the moment opportune for the conquest of Canada, and the diplomatic skill of Napoleon tipped the balance in favour of war and in favour of France. So the climax of the Napoleonic struggle was marked by a second Anglo-American war (1812–14) which widened a breach time had not filled.

Posterity has always regarded this war as needless and unhappy. Before it began, Great Britain had withdrawn the offending Orders in Council, and when it ended none of the disputed issues were settled. It took a course and had consequences unexpected by the combatants. While the American attempts on Canada were repulsed by the gallantry of its Loyalist and French Canadian inhabitants, the exploits of American frigates and privateers astonished the masters of the sea. In 1814 the British fleet harassed the Atlantic coast of America and raided Washington, but an army of Peninsular veterans under Sir Edward Pakenham, landed at New Orleans in December, suffered defeat at the hands of General Andrew Jackson. Unsought by Britain and unpopular in America, the war was brought to a speedy end, and though unknown in America, peace had been signed before Pakenham's defeat. The honours of the war belonged, for the most part, to the Canadians, but the young American nation was elated by its successes on the Atlantic and the lakes and by the victory at New Orleans, and gained in confidence and purpose, while General Jackson won a fame which carried him later to the White House. The Peace of Ghent in 1814 was as ineffectual as Jay's treaty in determining questions of neutral rights, but, like that treaty, it happily devised machinery for the settlement of boundary and other controversies.

It was a troubled world into which the American nation was born, and hard experiences formed the tradition of her policy. The long European wars obliged her to define her position. She successfully freed herself from dependence on England and France, asserted her separateness from the European system of politics and, having adopted neutrality, strove to the point of war for the maintenance of neutral rights. The Peace of 1783 had left the United States and Great Britain as neighbours with plenty of occasions for dispute, and both countries missed their opportunity when they allowed those occasions to cloud the prospects of their future relations. Then twenty years of war followed, in which Great Britain, with no effective weapon but her sea power, was certain to inflict the maximum of irritation on another maritime nation, little disposed in the circumstances to ask itself whether larger issues were not at stake than neutral trade. After 1814 Great Britain recognized that the United States had passed out of her colonial days and could no longer be treated as an old dependant, while America abandoned her attempt to acquire Canada by conquest. In 1818 an Anglo-American agreement to demilitarize the Canadian frontier bore witness to the hope and prospect of better relations between the three countries. The delimitation of Canadian-American boundaries was to make a long story, but henceforward of a diplomatic and not a military character.

In the New World America had won the battle for her position. Her own strength and Britain's maritime supremacy gave her security against the colonial ambitions of France. In North America she was dominant and regarded herself as heir of the waning colonial power of Spain. Events had indeed favoured her. Had Europe been at peace, or had France been victorious, she might have been deprived of her field of expansion before she was strong enough to secure it. European war, while it forced on her painful decisions and struggles, hurried her to the maturity of an independent status and gave her the opportunity of territorial growth.

So, by 1815, we see the new nation formed with its inheritance of English tradition; its unity achieved; its democratic government in successful operation and a vast field open for its growth. How would it realize its ambition to found a new order for mankind, exempt from European emergencies, in a New World?

# CHAPTER II

## Western Settlement

'What the Mediterranean sea was to the Greeks, breaking the bond of custom, offering new experiences, calling out new institutions and activities, that, and more, the ever-retreating frontier has been to the United States directly, and to the nations of Europe more remotely.'

F. J. TURNER: *The Significance of the Frontier in American History*

The America we know to-day is not the America of the Atlantic coast, which our forefathers planted, but a continental nation made on the great plains of the interior. The Constitution framed in 1787 still functions, though not in the manner contemplated by the Philadelphia Convention, but in accordance with ideas developed in the growth of American democracy. Throughout the greater part of the nineteenth century American energies were absorbed in the settlement of their immense territory. From ocean to ocean a democratic and industrial civilization was spread and the working of American institutions was adapted to the circumstances of an unprecedented national expansion.

In colonial days the French barred the way into the Mississippi valley. But at the Peace of Paris, 1763, France ceded to Great Britain Canada and all her lands between the Alleghany Mountains and the Mississippi. The Americans had helped to win these Western lands, which were the natural field of their expansion, and they were aggrieved when, in 1774, Great Britain annexed them to Canada for the purposes of the fur trade and closed them to settlement. In 1783 Great Britain agreed to hand them over to the United States, thus bringing the American boundary to the Mississippi. The delay in withdrawing our garrisons from the frontier posts which commanded the area was one of the causes of the ill-will which persisted between the two countries.

And an unjustified suspicion that Great Britain encouraged the Indian tribes to resist American pioneers there, for long excited a deep resentment in the West. Spain had received New Orleans and the remainder of Louisiana from France, and from her position at the mouth of the Mississippi she was able in the South to embarrass American expansion. From the beginning Spain regarded the growth of the United States with apprehension. 'A day will come', said Count Aranda in 1783, 'when [this new republic] will be a giant; she will then forget the favours that she has received...she will seize Florida and conquer New Spain.' Of its two neighbours Spain certainly was much more in the path of the growing nation than Great Britain and Count Aranda's prophecy was destined to fulfilment.

Americans always moved freely about their country in search of better opportunities. The Governor of Virginia wrote in 1772 of their restlessness: 'Wandering about seems engrafted in their nature'; they 'for ever imagine the lands further off are still better than those upon which they are already settled.'[1] Abraham Lincoln's family, for example, emigrated from England to Massachusetts in 1638; thence they moved South, trying their fortunes in New Jersey, Pennsylvania and Virginia. The spirit that carried the father across the Atlantic carried the son into the forest and the Alleghany Mountains. Before the War of Independence the first stockaded settlements were planted on the Western streams. The Indians were a danger and stockades were necessary for defence: in 1780 Lincoln's grandfather was murdered by Indians on his Virginian farm. All along the border small bands of settlers were on the move. Hard times and dislike of restraint impelled some; curiosity and love of adventure lured others. The movement was spontaneous. State governments neither initiated nor controlled it. To the blue grass prairies of Kentucky and to Central Tennessee 100,000 persons had come by 1789. It was clear that America was going to grow and to grow fast, and the Continental Congress, in its famous North-West Terri-

[1] Morison, S. E. and Commager, H. S., *American Republic*, I, 22.

torial Ordinance of 1787, made provision for the future self-government of the West. The new land should be filled with a free people. As the land was occupied an area called a Territory was formed, to which a limited self-government was given, and when a part of this was ripe for statehood, with a population not less than 60,000, a new State was created which was admitted to the Union on the same footing as the old. The mother was to have an equal brood.

The Western territories were, as we have seen, transferred to the national government out of the hands of the States. A single control was necessary. In a new country the disposal of public lands is a vital matter. Lord Durham, in his famous *Report on Canada*, writes: 'Upon the manner in which this business is conducted it may almost be said that everything else depends.'[1] Was the land to be granted out in large areas or small holdings? Was the West to be exploited by the capitalist and speculator or reserved for the real settlers? Would occupation be discouraged till the old States filled up? Eastern employers did not want to lose their labour. There were different points of view. The Congress of 1796 which decided the matter focused their policy on the principle of rapid settlement. The interest of the nation, it was held, was to plant as many citizens as possible in the West rather than to hoard land for higher prices—to make it the people's home rather than the business man's capital. Expanding settlement would strengthen the United States and would anticipate any attempt of England, France or Spain to recover their possessions.

The Government very quickly developed an admirable system for dealing with the land, and no Government has been more successful in getting the land into the hands of genuine settlers—men who would occupy, cultivate and improve their holdings—which is the test of a good land policy in a new country. In Canada at this time the British Government was far less successful, as Lord Durham lamented. For the most part the Government

[1] *Report on Canada* (Edition 1902), p. 144.

dealt direct with the settler and not through Land Companies; it sold by auction at a low upset price, up to 1820 of $2 an acre, and thereafter of $1.25; it gave a freehold title and, later (1841), recognized the squatter's right of pre-emption. Large grants were also made to the States for public purposes, such as roads and education, and, later on, to railway companies, but with less satisfactory results.

'The system of the United States', wrote Lord Durham in 1838,[1] 'appears to combine all the chief requisites of the greatest efficiency. It is uniform throughout the vast federation;...it renders the acquisition of new land easy and yet, by means of a price, restricts appropriation to the actual wants of the settler; it is so simple as to be readily understood; it provides for accurate surveys and against needless delays; it gives an instant and secure title; and it admits of no favouritism, but distributes the public property amongst all classes of persons upon precisely equal terms. That system has promoted an amount of immigration and settlement, of which the history of the world affords no other example....'

The West was indeed making phenomenal progress. Unemployment in the East during the European wars sent out successive waves of settlers. By 1815 the Westerners numbered two millions, and five new States, Vermont, Kentucky, Tennessee, Ohio and Louisiana, had been admitted to the Union. The needs of the West were becoming the chief concern of the politicians in Washington and its voice had been heard in foreign policy, when Henry Clay and his war-hawks voted for the war of 1812. Along the Gulf of Mexico cotton plantations were spreading and in the Ohio valley the settlers were struggling with the forest. Abraham Lincoln's father was amongst the pioneers in this region. He had followed the westward trend of population from Virginia to Kentucky, the first State formed beyond the mountains (1792), and Lincoln himself was born there in 1809, on a poor Western farm, bought on credit and only slowly paid for.

[1] *Report on Canada*, p. 148.

In 1816 his father hears of richer land in Indiana; so he builds a flat boat, floats it down the Rolling Fork and the Ohio to Thompson's Ferry. Sixteen miles from the river, at Pigeon Creek, he finds a settlement beginning, some eight or ten families arriving. He chooses a location, sells the boat, which could not be floated up stream, walks back to Kentucky, and brings his family to Pigeon Creek in waggons.

Then follows the battle with nature. The settlers barter their produce for cloth and shot at the village store. Soon there is a cargo of corn to be floated down to New Orleans. People could cross the mountains, but heavy goods could not, and that was why the free navigation of the Mississippi mattered so much to the West. As the settlers came, if they succeeded, which was not always the case, business grew, the store abandoned barter and did a trade of thousands of dollars in merchandise and produce, and the forest gave place to a group of villages like Pigeon Creek settlement. Labour the settlers provided for themselves, helping one another and creating the tradition of American neighbourliness; capital was hard to find, and the West resented the control of credit exerted by the moneyed East.

If you returned after a decade to one of these regions where settlement was succeeding, the forest had given place to farms, with crops of maize and wheat, little hamlets were becoming towns and the streams were alive with boats. Lumber, grain, hemp and pork went down the river to the settlers along the Gulf of Mexico. The purchase of Louisiana in 1803 and of Florida in 1819 had ended at last the difficulties with Spain; and the Mississippi had become an American river. Towns were growing up at points of vantage for the exchange of farm produce with manufactured articles—first at river junctions, later at railway centres. A growing town presented an extraordinary spectacle, with a central core of good buildings—houses, hotels and factories—surrounded by a straggling circle of wooden huts and shanties.

As the Western settlements grew, the question of transport

became vital. Western farmers wanted to sell produce in Eastern towns and Eastern manufacturers to send their goods to the Western farmers. Otherwise, East and West would fall apart and even their political union be threatened. It was thought that high roads should be built to connect East and West, and in 1808 a great system of national roads was planned, though only one, the Cumberland Road or National Pike, was built, which connected Washington with Illinois. Canals, too, were envisaged to link up the river system. The invention of the steamboat came opportunely. In 1809 the first steamboat was built on the River Hudson and within a few years steamers were bringing a new life to the Mississippi valley.

The Western settlers were clamouring for roads, canals, harbours—internal improvements of all kinds. But they lacked capital for large enterprises. Had the National Government the right to undertake this kind of work? The Westerners, who would get the advantage of it, and those who thought to increase the power and popularity of the National Government by making it a fountain of benefits, maintained that it had. Strict constructionists in the Eastern States, which had more capital and less need of improvements, thought not. But gradually the National Government drifted into a vast programme of public works, justified on one pretext or another. This was called Clay's American System. Henry Clay, a forceful politician from Kentucky, made himself the spokesman of the material interests of the Middle West—protection and improvements—and exerted great influence in this period of growth. As the various Western communities were competing with each other for national aid, political jobbery and log-rolling was rampant in Congress. Meanwhile State Governments became active, particularly in canal construction, and discovered that they could borrow in Europe. The most important of the canals was the Erie Canal (1817–25), which linked the western parts of New York State with the Atlantic and gave the city of New York its great start as an outlet for Western trade.

While democracy was thus being planted in the Mississippi valley, a considerable issue of foreign policy, affecting the future of the American Republic, was coming to a head. During the European war, Spanish America had slipped away from the mother land. When the war ended the great question was posed: was Spain to recover her colonies or would they now become independent, as a large part of their inhabitants desired? The Holy Alliance was disposed to come to the help of Spain against her revolting colonies. The position of the United States was very different from what it had been thirty years before. In North America she had inherited much of the falling colonial empire of Spain and she was strong enough to take decisive action. Though not very sanguine that the Latin colonists would make good republicans, she was happy to see her example spreading its influence through the New World, and was determined that the monarchies of Europe should not intervene to settle its destinies. On this matter of the Spanish colonies Great Britain and the United States were in substantial agreement and for a moment the two nations trembled on the verge of an alliance. The aged Jefferson, who was consulted, advised action with Great Britain: 'with her on our side we need not fear the whole world'. But the American Government knew that they would get British support without paying this unpopular price. So in the end the two countries did not act together. But they acted alike, and American strength and British maritime power combined to secure the independence of the New World. America gave recognition to the new States in 1822 and President Monroe, in his famous message to Congress the following year, took the opportunity to make a general declaration on American policy.

Our policy in regard to Europe, he said, is not to take part in purely European wars, nor to interfere in the internal concerns of any European power. In regard to these continents 'it is impossible that the Allied Powers should extend their political system to any portion of either continent without endangering our peace and happiness', nor should we view their intervention with indifference. Further, the American continents, being now free and independent, 'are henceforth not to be considered as subjects for future colonisation by any European Powers'.

British ministers had hoped to call in the New World to redress the balance of the Old, but Monroe's policy was to make the New World safe for American democracy and to keep it out of the balances of the Old. Action by a European state on the American continents might endanger the security or interests of the United States, and to prevent it he would separate the New World politically from the Old. Washington's policy of withdrawing America from the European system received its complement in Monroe's policy of warning off Europe from the American system. It was a declaration of great significance, explaining America's sense of her external interests and her general outlook in foreign policy.

Washington and Jefferson had formulated the principle of America's separation from European policy. But for thirty years after her independence historic connections and great events had interwoven her affairs with the struggle in Europe. The fall of Napoleon and the decline of her external trade diminished her interests abroad, and with the growth of the West, her sense of aloofness from Europe became stronger. Her chief concern now was with her internal affairs—the expansion of settlement with all its activities and problems. Economic issues commanded the political field—communications, banking, industry and the tariff—and the controversies that arose out of them, like the right of Congress to charter a national bank and the right of a State to nullify a federal Act. The affairs of Europe seemed far away and awoke little interest. Its national and liberal movements America regarded with sympathy, but with detachment. She made no foreign alliance and seldom entered into common action with European powers. The ocean steamer (1838) and the electric telegraph (1844) were soon to begin their silent knitting of new ties with other lands. But these things and their consequences lay in the future. Meanwhile a deep-rooted sense of separation from the troubles and interests of the Old World settled upon her and became one of the strongest of her political instincts. For the greater part of the century events continued to strengthen it.

At the same time a strong national feeling was developing and American self-confidence grew by leaps and bounds. The great experiment had succeeded and democracy was finding full expression in a large state. The West grew continuously; by 1821 the thirteen states had become twenty-four and the population of the country exceeded ten millions. The growth of the West was producing a new American type; its opportunities filled the popular mind; its needs were the principal concern of the country and its expansive spirit was forcing the hands of Government. The idea of America for the Americans had appeared.

In 1830 the advancing tide of settlement was half-way across the continent. Pioneers were pushing beyond the forests on to the prairie that spread westwards like an ocean before them. From Louisiana explorers had already made trails into the far West and come down on the Pacific shore. To the north the British and American Governments had in 1818 agreed on a joint occupation of the country known as Oregon between Spanish territory and Russian Alaska. To the south American settlers were pushing into Texas, a Mexican province, large as France, rich in prairie and forest; caravans of American traders went annually to Santa Fé in New Mexico, and a few Americans, coming by sea or overland, had already made their way to California. In the 'forties the Oregon fever touched the frontiersmen of Missouri and the advancing tide of settlement gave a leap to the Pacific coast. It was a long trail, 1500 miles, up the Missouri and the Platte, by the South Pass, through the arid basin of Wyoming, and down the Columbia to the fertile valleys which the American missions had discovered. But the 'prairie schooner', the covered waggon, could make it. In organized parties of 100 waggons, with their cattle, the pioneers sallied forth. Not all got through, but, by 1845, 8000 Americans were settled on the Columbia and the United States demanded a decision of the Oregon frontier. Great

Britain had claimed the River Columbia as her boundary, while President Polk held that the United States had a title to the whole of the territory. Both receded from their claims, and by agreement in 1846 the country was divided along the 49th parallel, which Adams had offered to Castlereagh in 1818. It gave to America a wide Pacific frontier and left to Canada her future province of British Columbia. Four years earlier the Ashburton-Webster treaty settled the boundary question between New Brunswick and Maine. These two treaties were compromises of long-standing differences, wisely accepted by both nations for the sake of peace and friendship.

Meanwhile, to the south, Texas, on its own application, was admitted to the Union in 1845 and, war with Mexico following, New Mexico and California were annexed in 1848. The Southerners wanted lands into which their peculiar institution could be carried in order to balance the growing North, and statesmen had grounds for their fear that unless Texas became American, England and France would make of her a buffer state to check American expansion. The United States was in the full tide of its westward advance and public opinion responded to the orators who proclaimed transcontinental expansion as 'manifest destiny'. But the rivalry of the sections set some check on the expansive spirit, for northern growth was not popular in the South, nor southern in the North.

These acquisitions of the 'forties virtually completed the territorial growth of the United States. In the course of thirty years Spain had been eliminated from North America, the advance of Russia down the Pacific coast checked, the boundaries of Canada defined, Oregon divided with Britain, and large cessions of territory, exacted from Mexico, had rounded off the continental area and given to the United States its commanding position as a Pacific power. Though Southern politicians might still hanker after Cuba, most Americans were now satisfied. The United States had reached its natural or agreed frontiers. In Latin America her aim was not territory or domination, but the exclu-

sion of European political influence, and in this connection the
Clayton-Bulwer treaty of 1850 diminished the dangers of future
differences with Great Britain. The two powers agreed that
neither would ever obtain exclusive control over a future Panama
canal or occupy or colonize any part of Central America. Palmerston's interpretation of the treaty and William Walker's activities
in Nicaragua aroused some mutual suspicion in the following
decade, but the disputes were compromised. In the Caribbean
area, Great Britain, recognizing America's superior interests,
definitely accepted the *status quo* and sought no further expansion.
'With the existing colonies or dependencies of any European
Power', Monroe had said, 'we have not interfered and shall not
interfere', though the hope that Canada would throw in her lot
with the United States lived on in many American minds till
recent times.

Settlers were soon pushing into the new areas. In the 'forties
the Mormons had started their westward pilgrimage, and in 1848,
under the vigorous leadership of Brigham Young, they established a successful colony in the region of the Great Salt Lake.
Suddenly, 'the flashing and golden pageant' of California came
into view and a rush began to the Pacific coast. The Middle West
gave its pioneers to the Overland Trail. Companies of emigrants
formed themselves, with their waggons, mules and oxen, for the
transcontinental journey. These were the 'forty-niners'. The
gold fever subsided, but the limitless expanse of prairie stretched
before the settler and Kansas and Nebraska drew the stream.
Emigrant waggons passed across the northern States with the
words Kansas and Nebraska chalked on their canvas coverings,
the settlers carrying their rifles in their hands and their ploughs
and sickles in the baggage. To the north, the spring wheat lands
of Minnesota, reaching to the Canadian border, were coming
under occupation, and, farther west, mining camps were spring-
ing up in the foothills of the Rockies. The miner revealed the
resources of the far West to the rancher and the farmer, and by
the Homestead Act of 1862 Congress set the crown on its land

policy by giving a 'quarter section', 160 acres, to the genuine
settler. The free home in the West was a new magnet to the
settler, whose force was to be felt when the Civil War ended.
Meanwhile, industrial development on an increasing scale offered
a field of employment to European immigrants and swelled the
population of the North Atlantic States and New England. Over
the whole country population had grown from under 10 millions
in 1820 to over 17 in 1840 and 31½ in 1860, by which date
twenty new States had been admitted into the Union.

The success of this great movement of people was due, in the
first instance, to the fact that the eastern colonies formed a strong
base, adjoining the scene, from which colonization could pro-
ceed. Colonization requires capital and labour and it requires
the right kind of labour. First must come the pioneer to blaze
the trail, and the best men for that are men familiar with the
country. The pioneer finds water, clears the wood, erects a log
cabin and then, when neighbours crowd around, sells out and
moves on. The lumberer, the rancher or the farmer follow and
in their turn sell out to men of capital and enterprise and the
small villages grow into towns, as wave after wave of emigrants
rolls westward. The Atlantic colonies were large and populous
enough to provide the various kinds of labour that were required
as settlement progressed. American colonization was an internal
movement of population. From the beginning the East made
the West, and the East was not only a source of labour and
capital, but in due course a market for the produce of the West.
The East became industrial, while the West was still agricultural, and economically the two parts of the country were com-
plementary to each other. The developing East was ever feeding
the needs of the expanding West.

The supply of labour came not only from the Eastern States,
but after 1815 from Europe also. Until within recent years the
United States opened its doors wide to the European immigrant
and never doubted its capacity to make him a good American.
The expanding field of employment, the high wages and better

chances in life were very attractive to the multitudes who were suffering from industrial and agrarian changes in Europe and from political persecution. From 1830 the Catholic Irish began to come in large numbers, and during the next twenty years, which included the years of famine in Ireland, 1846 and 1847, they formed nearly half of the total immigration. By 1850 there were nearly one million Irish in the United States. The year of revolution, 1848, stimulated the exodus from Europe, particularly from Germany. Down to 1860 the stream flowed from the northern countries—from Great Britain and Ireland, from Germany, France and Scandinavia, and more than five million immigrants entered the United States, to become citizens and usually Democrats. The immigrants, however, did not lead the westward movement; chiefly they provided the labour supply for the expanding industries in the North Atlantic States, for mining and railway construction; they did the heavier and lower work of the country. The native American element kept the leadership and control. Nor did the immigrants go into the South; there was no demand for their labour where slavery existed. In years of depression the stream would slacken, swelling again with the return of good times. But always there was this flowing tide of population, urging forward the expansion of America and building up its gigantic strength.

Another factor in the extension of settlement was the demand for raw materials in Europe as industrialization progressed. There was a market beyond the seas as well as at home for all the West could produce. Inventions of agricultural machinery stimulated production, improvement in transport lowered the cost of carriage on land and sea, so that the food and the raw materials of the West could find their way to British ports. Never were conditions more favourable for the growth of a new country. Between 1840 and 1860 the production of maize and wheat and tobacco was doubled and of cotton almost trebled.

The improvements in transport were vital to expansion. After the Indian danger was ended and when the settlers had passed from the forest on to the prairie, distance had become the great obstacle to the progress of the West. But what roads and canals could not do, the railway could; and it was the railway that was to solve the problem of communications and transport for the growing country. Distance was no longer an obstacle, nor the mountain barrier, and the railway could go where there were no rivers. The railway supplied the means for the exchange of commodities between the Atlantic cities and the Mississippi valley; it knit them together economically and so preserved their political unity.

The first railway was built in 1828. Soon railways radiated from the Atlantic ports and were built through to the nearer points in the West. By 1853 more than 6000 miles had been constructed, by 1860 more than 30,000. Railways linked up the Eastern cities, joined them to the Western settlements and carried the minerals to the industrial centres. Their rapid multiplication was due to the general enthusiasm with which the invention was received. States, counties, towns, individuals, all combined to speed construction. The financial difficulty was overcome when someone suggested the idea of bond and mortgage. By this expedient the initial cost was funded and the railway could live while it was getting up a traffic. Railways were never considered fit subjects for national aid, apart from the grant of land, nor was it now needed; for this expedient made possible the great railway development that followed.

As the tide of settlement moved across the country it created an ever-moving frontier. This frontier, of course, was not along one line. Wherever there was unsettled land there was a frontier line and frontier influences, and there were many frontier districts in the eastern States long after much of the West was settled. So the influences exerted by the frontier on American life were not localized and did not make for sectionalism. Nor was the frontier of a single type. Between the old settled areas and the Indian frontier, where the pioneers struggled with the red man and the pitiless winter for existence, were various intermediate states—the farmer's frontier, with its problems of land, labour and transport, the rancher's frontier, with its isolation, and beyond them, the miner's frontier, with its special problems of law and order. These different conditions mingled their influences on the life of the country. But from 1850 the prairie farmer and not the backwoodsman was becoming the typical pioneer.

The spirit of the frontier was free and masterful. It ignored the accepted standards and social training of the East. In its hard conditions self-reliance was necessary and only efficiency counted. Wealth was respected if hospitable, education if useful, birth if public-spirited. The life took heavy toll of human strength, but it bred a realism and an impatient energy which passed into the American character. Men who succeeded in the West had confidence in themselves. And if all men were created equal, they did not see why they should not have an equal control in politics. Already the West had made itself felt both in domestic and foreign policy. In the 'twenties it took the control of national politics out of the hands of the Eastern leaders and asserted itself in the election of Andrew Jackson as President (1828)—the first President from a Western State.

The fathers of the Constitution never intended the people to choose the President. The Constitution provided that the President should be chosen by a special College appointed by the States. This electoral body still exists, but it was still-born. It has never once chosen the President. Washington was the obvious choice in 1788 and 1792, and when he refused a further nomination, the two parties which had come into existence had each their leader, the Federalists, John Adams, and the Democratic-Republicans, Thomas Jefferson, and they in turn were chosen. After that, until 1824, caucuses of members of Congress told the College of Electors for whom to vote. At the election of 1824 no candidate had the required majority and the House of Representatives, in accordance with the Constitution, had to appoint, and they chose John Quincy Adams, who had the support of the greater number of States, and passed over

Andrew Jackson, who had the largest popular vote. A great cry arose that the sovereign will of the people had been disregarded. This was a new sound in American politics and it came from the West. At the next election the people took the choice of the party candidates out of the hands of members of Congress and created a new machinery for the purpose—the Nominating Convention.

Jackson was elected and the West saw him into the White House. For hours was heard the crash of glass as Jackson's guests celebrated their victory. The sovereign people was a little uproarious, said a newspaper the next day, but it was in anything but a malicious spirit.

Since this time the party candidates and the party programme have been decided by the Nominating Convention of each party. The party managers amalgamate the sectional claims into a party programme and choose as party candidate the most 'available' man, viz. the man who is likely to collect the largest number of votes. It was a great act of political assertion by the new democracy, but it brought politics under the control of the professional politicians who ran the Conventions and lowered the tone of political life. The educated classes tended to withdraw. Except in great crises, it was difficult to nominate a national leader for the Presidency. John Quincy Adams in 1824 was the last President chosen for merit and not for political 'availability'. Various influences combined with the change to degrade political life and to bring about in the great republic that contrast between the low tone of politics and the high private character of the people, which throughout a great part of the nineteenth century all observers were to note. American politics now exhibited that corruption which had made them so distrustful and disdainful of the British Parliamentary system a century before.

The 'era of good feelings', when there were no political parties and the early problems had all found an agreed solution, was ended by the rapid growth of the West. In the political field

Henry Clay represented its material interests and Jackson its democratic spirit. After the election of 1824 they parted company and the Democratic Republicans divided behind them. Clay's followers now formed a new party which picked up again the traditions of the Federalists and took the name of National Republicans and, later, of Whigs. The other group dropped the word 'Republican' from the old title and became the Democratic party, which has had a continuous existence since and is in power to-day. The Democrats, Emerson said, had the best principles and the Whigs the best men.[1] But the Democrats, who, in Jackson's time, were a national party with strong support in North and West, took up the cause of State rights, and gradually passed under the control of the Southern leaders, to become the instrument of the slaveowners. For a long time, however, the leaders of both parties did their best to keep the issue of slavery out of politics.

Old Hickory, as Andrew Jackson was called, had the vehemence and the simplicity of the West. The people had sent him to the White House to carry democratic ideas into politics and he intended to do it. He brought into national government the theory that any American citizen is fit for any political or administrative post to which he may be called, that training and experience are not essential in the sphere of administration. Rotation in office, he said in his Presidential message, is a principle of the Republican creed. Palmerston's remark that an English gentleman is capable of any job that he has the influence to get was given its democratic form. Jefferson had made changes in the Civil Service, but Jackson made a wholesale sweep in order to put in his supporters—a process since called the Spoils System. He had to reward his party-men, and, as Webster said, the multitude was so great that it could not be fed without a miracle. From this time for many years every holder of an administrative post was liable to, if not certain of, discharge on a change of the party in power. Jackson did not invent the system. It existed in the State of New York

[1] Morison, II, 29.

and he transplanted it to the National Government. He thought the Civil Service dishonest and, as the people wanted it reformed, he sacked the lot. It was a national result of the democratic revolution. But it mixed up administration with politics, and the consequent insecurity of tenure lowered the standard of men who desired to enter the Civil Service.

The West made itself felt also in economic policy. Its ideas and interests differed from those of the settled parts and produced a constant struggle in the political arena. The Westerners wanted land, labour and capital, the great agents of production, to be as fluid and as serviceable to them as possible. They wanted land sold cheap or given away, while the East would have kept up the price. The West wanted protection for raw produce, the East for manufactures. The West wanted the National Government to help it develop its great heritage and to provide roads and canals and other internal improvements, while the East did not wish to see national activities and powers enlarged in this way. The West wanted an easy banking system, cheap money, plenty of notes, and, later on, the free coinage of silver and no control by big financiers; the East wanted a strongly controlled banking system and the gold standard. Financial questions were a battlefield all through American history. In these years of growth there was a spirit of speculative enterprise always seeking to extend the channels of credit. There seemed so many opportunities, all needing capital, and very little capital available. Hamilton had tried to give the country a good start, but the Constitution gave insufficient power to the National Government in matters of finance. So the United States has had a chequered financial history—an eager unscrupulous energy constantly running away with the control and bringing the country to a series of financial crises. Hamilton's policy of a national bank might have steadied the course of development and controlled the supply of credit. But the bank's control was unpopular in the West and in 1811 its charter was not extended. The 'era of good feelings' produced agreement even on this question and a second U.S. bank was founded in 1815. The West looked on the B.U.S., as it was called, as an aristocratic and tyrannical institution, which kept the people from developing their heritage. Jackson shared their idea —that the money power was the enemy of democracy. 'I do not dislike your bank more than all banks', he informed the President of the B.U.S. 'But ever since I read the history of the South Sea Bubble, I have been afraid of banks.'[1] So in 1832 he vetoed the re-charter, as an unconstitutional invasion of State rights and a monopoly making profits in favour of foreign stockholders and a few hundred Americans chiefly of the richest class. American democracy hated monopoly and rejoiced in Jackson's economics. So Hamilton's idea finally failed. The State banks stepped in to fill the void. They gave the West what it wanted—easy credit, and the West used it, as was to be expected, with a speculative energy that produced the financial crises of 1837 and 1857. The National Government was forced to adopt the inelastic system of an Independent Treasury, to keep its own funds and mind its own business, and the economic development of the U.S.A. went forward without a central financial control.

With the expansion of the country, its different regions began to take a distinctive character. New England, more closely settled and more English in its traditions than other parts, retained its intellectual leadership. Its commercial importance declined, but its industries expanded and it was still the centre of literary and educational life. The Middle States formed an intermediate area between New England and the South and between the East and the West, partaking of the character of all parts. They grew greatly because they stretched into the West, whereas New England did not, and they had also mineral resources. They were more national in their ideas than other parts of the East. The South preserved the separate outlook which the institution of slavery had given it. As cotton cultivation spread west, its old aristocracy gave place to the great cotton planters. Economically and politically it felt a solidity of interest

[1] Morison and Commager, I, 382.

and an aloofness from the North. The interests of the two sections were intertwined, but their views were different. The North financed, admired and to some extent educated the South, which, in its turn, respected the wealth, learning and civilized comfort of the North, but despised its social and religious life. The two sections of the country diverged more and more. The vast region of pioneers beyond the mountains was dividing into two parts as both North and South extended their different life into the West. The North-Western States resembled the Middle States, with great cities rising up as centres of industry and communications, while the South-Western States followed their Southern neighbours.

Industrial development was now coming to enhance the sectional differences. The War of Independence was not immediately followed by large industrial changes. For twenty years America grew fast, without changing in character. There was no sign of an industrial revolution. It was not British colonial policy that had checked the rise of manufacturing industries. The European war (1793–1815) destroyed the profits of trade and increased the profits of industry. Capital and labour were turned to manufactures. By 1815 there was a cotton industry in New England, a woollen industry in Massachusetts and an iron industry in Pennsylvania. The country lost its colonial and purely rural character and began to show signs of its future industrial greatness. All the factories were in the North. The South was not to be industrial. That was clear at once. Slavery could not supply skilled and intelligent labour. So the economic sectionalism became more definite. With the growth of industry came a demand for protective legislation and the protectionists won their first victory in the tariff of 1816.

The stronghold of protection was in the Middle and Western States, where the farmers were asking for duties on wool, hemp, flax and even grain. In New England the commercial interest favoured free trade, while the South wanted cheap food and clothes for the slaves, and from the first set its face against protection. So each tariff was a struggle. The South felt that they bore the burden of protection and that the North got all its benefits. They wanted free trade and slave labour, the North free labour and protected industries.

The industrial revolution came gradually in the U.S.A. All through this period of growth the chief interest of the country was in agriculture. The competition of cheap land and an independent career was too much for the manufacturers, raising, as it did, the price of labour. The great industrial expansion of the country came later when the competition of other occupations was less strong and cheaper labour was pouring in from Europe. But the industrial growth added its stimulus to the demand for cheap transport, for the manufacturers wanted to sell their goods in the West and also needed the development of transport to link up ore fields and manufacturing centres.

In general the influences of Western life worked in favour of national unity and against sectionalism. On the frontier, people were always moving, moving from place to place and from occupation to occupation, in search of better chances. Moreover, they mixed more freely with each other and had more in common than in the older areas. Men of all States and different nations met and mingled. On the frontier the composite nationality of America was forming. Here took shape also a new idea of the Union. For the idea that the Union was an agreement between independent states was substituted the idea that it was an indissoluble union of the people. This idea came easily to the West, for its settlers represented the new American nation, drawn from all parts of the country and from Europe and consolidating in the vast interior of the continent. They were not less democratic than their ancestors, but whereas in Jefferson's day American democracy was instinct with the spirit of local independence, in Jackson's it was national. They were loyal to the Constitution, but they were determined to work it in their own way. The federal system, too, allowed of local variety, and State constitutions were a safety valve where the democratic spirit could find its outlet and make its political experiments. If the Western politicians broke down the conservative traditions of Washington, they strengthened the National Government. Their impatient energy worked for good and ill in national politics, but it did not divide the country. They made American democracy and the American nation and, when later these were threatened, they thought them worth preserving. It was the West which turned the scales between North and South.

American life might be raw and awkward, but it was tolerant and kindly. Social intercourse was easy and pleasant, for it lacked the stiffening of class divisions. A growing spirit of humanitarianism found its most vigorous expression amongst the abolitionists of the North. Interest in education was growing, and from Illinois came the demand for a system of higher education adapted to the needs of the industrial classes, which was to bear fruit in the Land Grant Act of 1862 providing for the endowment of industrial education in all the States. Apart from education, to which American democracy had already pinned its faith, there was little idea, as yet, of using the Government to effect social purposes. A self-reliant people, with the open opportunities of the West, preferred to fend for themselves. No Factory Act was passed by any State before the Civil War, except to regulate the working hours of children and so ensure to them the chance of education. There was 'a free church, a free school, free land, a free vote and a free career for the child of the humblest' and the nation was satisfied, and felt, and boisterously asserted, the superiority of its circumstances over those of the Old World. The state of growth, with its hopes and fears and pains and expanding horizons, was highly stimulating and put a spirit of youth into everything. If the West concentrated on material things, there was intellectual distinction in New England, where philosophy, poetry and fiction placed the achievements of American life on the universal plane. Emerson gave to democracy a spiritual significance, and Hawthorne and Herman Melville were masters of fiction. In poetry Longfellow wrote what his generation most liked to read, but it was Whitman who sang of democracy and the Union—

These States are the amplest poem—

and of the occupations of the ordinary man:

> In the labour of engines and trades
> and the labour of the fields
> I find the developments
> And find the eternal meanings.

The Westerners, intent on their own affairs, were little conscious of all this. But, with all their drawbacks, 'the Northern and Western States were a land where dreams of youth came true; where the vast majority of men were doing what they wished to do, without restraint by class or administration.... Half the population were engaged in realizing the ambition of frustrated peasant ancestors for a farm of their very own, clear of rent and charges. The other half, having achieved the farm, had tired of it; and...had turned to some other occupation or taken up pioneering again.'[1] To the under-dog of Western civilization America offered a free home, free government and a fresh chance. In the Old World many of the upper class saw with apprehension and jealousy the success of the American experiment, but democrats hailed in it the fulfilment of Turgot's prediction, 'This people is the hope of the human race', and deduced from it new arguments for reforms at home.

Such was America in the making; when in the full tide of its expansion disaster fell upon it and disunion threatened the great republic.

[1] Morison, I, 418.

# CHAPTER III

## *The Union*

'Both parties deprecated war; but one of them would make war rather than let the nation survive, and the other would accept war rather than let it perish.'

ABRAHAM LINCOLN: *The Second Inaugural Address* (March 4, 1865)

While the Mississippi valley was being occupied and American democracy developing, a deep-seated problem of a political, social and moral character was gradually dividing opinion throughout the country and so seriously as to threaten the continuance of the Union. It was always possible to take different views of the nature and purpose of the Union. It was possible to argue that it was an agreement between independent States, voluntarily entered into, and that any State could therefore, if it thought fit, withdraw. It may be that in 1789 a majority of Americans thought this. But when, in 1860, this issue was brought to the test, the majority of Americans rejected that view and fought a great war to maintain the indissoluble character of the Union. In their conviction the nation was consolidated in one political community and sovereignty belonged not to the individual States but to the whole people.

From the beginning of the Union there occurred from time to time the sharpest division of opinion concerning some proposed action of the National Government, and State rights—that is the right of a State to oppose the action of the National Government—had been vehemently and even menacingly asserted. In 1798 two of the fathers of the republic, both destined to be Presidents of the United States, Jefferson and Madison, had maintained that States could refuse to obey, that is nullify, an Act of the Federal Government, if, in their judgment, that Government was exceeding its powers. And they persuaded their

respective state legislatures, Kentucky and Virginia, to pass resolu-
tions to that effect, directed against the Alien and Sedition Acts of
that year. But these Acts were soon after repealed and the trouble
passed. Later, the war of 1812 stirred feeling so strongly in New
England that there was talk of secession and again a threat to
nullify a federal Act. But wiser counsels prevailed and this trouble
too passed. More serious was the opposition of some of the
Southern States to the tariff of 1828. Andrew Jackson was President at the time; he was a native of South Carolina, a Democrat
and supposed to be a State rights man. The Southerners hoped
to enlist him on their side and invited him in April 1830 to an
anniversary dinner to celebrate Jefferson's birthday. Asked to
give a toast, he gave 'Our Union—it must be preserved'.
Calhoun, Vice-President of the United States, the leader of the
South, answered this challenge with another, 'The Union—next
to our liberty, the most dear'. So the sides were taken. South
Carolina then summoned a Convention which declared the
Tariff Act null and void and not binding on the State or its
citizens. Jackson declared that the power to annul a law was
incompatible with the existence of the Union and he asked
Congress for a Revenue Collection Bill, or Force Act, as the
Southerners called it, in order to give effect to the law. But
Henry Clay, the great maker of compromises, managed to adjust
the dispute; the tariff was modified and the storm subsided.
Again the issue had been compromised and the question of State
rights left unsettled.

By that time forty years had passed since the Constitution had
been framed and hesitatingly accepted. A new generation had
come into being and a new America. The contest made it clear
that the Union commanded the faith and allegiance of the country,
which regarded it as no temporary dwelling house, but as the
birthplace and home of the nation. America's greatest orator,
Daniel Webster, extolled the Union in speeches which all
Americans read and still read. 'Liberty first and Union afterwards' he declared to be 'words of delusion and folly': 'to

every true American heart—liberty and union' were 'now and for ever, one and inseparable'.[1]

He spoke the sentiment forming in the hearts of the Northern and Western people and still of many in the South. Conditions had changed since 1789 and men's ideas and feelings had changed with them. The growing needs of the country, the extended powers of the National Government, the increasing number of States, had brought about new conditions in which the Union meant far more to the country than it had meant in 1789. Trade, transport and currency were no longer local questions, but national concerns. The expansion of settlement had enlarged the duties of the Government and political centralization had followed the economic growth. A national political consciousness had been born. The progress and prosperity of the nation, its secure position in the world, were eloquent of the advantages of union.

In the increase of the powers of the Federal Government the action of the Supreme Court in the interpretation of the Constitution had been of the greatest importance. The words of the Constitution were general and everything depended on how they were construed. If the Court construed them precisely, the Government would not have the power to meet the needs of a growing country. Between 1801 and 1835 one judge, Chief Justice Marshall, presided continuously over the Court, and he did more, probably, than any other man to shape the powers of the National Government. He held that the Constitution must be interpreted as a living organism, that it was not a treaty to be strictly construed, but a group of rules to be continually expanded in meaning to meet changing conditions. He argued that the creation of the National Government implied the grant to it not only of the powers named in the Constitution, but of all subsidiary powers necessary to make the named powers effective: that the Government had discretion as to the means it used in doing its work. 'Let the end be legitimate', he said in a famous

[1] Morison, I, 394.

case concerning the Bank of the United States (1819), 'and all
means which are appropriate, plainly adapted to that end and
not prohibited, are constitutional.' Thus the power to collect
taxes implied the power to impose a protective tariff, the power
to borrow money implied the power to charter a national bank,
the power to regulate trade implied the powers to assist public
works and regulate interstate transport, and the power to declare
war implied the power to do the multitude of things which a
state of war necessitated.

Not less important had been the creation of the new States.
The new States strengthened the National Government, because
they were its children and not its parents, they were made by
it and did not make it, as the original States had done, and they
felt a loyalty the older States did not feel. They had no traditions
of independent existence, and consequently no such strong local
feelings as the separate existence of colonial days had fostered in
their Atlantic neighbours. They wanted the National Government to help them and so they had no wish to restrain its powers.
In their vast area the National Government was looked up to
with gratitude as the fountain of benefit and as the sovereign
authority.

Thus when the most serious strain which it had yet borne was
placed upon the Union, its hold upon the affections of the people
and the powers of the National Government were very different
from what they had been in 1789. This strain arose from the
increasing tension between the different sections of the country
which the institution of slavery had long been causing. As we
have seen, the Union began its existence with this latent problem.
At that time most Americans hoped that slavery would disappear
and thought it would die a natural death, and in static conditions
the problem need never have threatened the unity of the country.
But conditions were never static in the United States. Movements of opinion and movements of population were continuous
and they had steadily aggravated the problem. One by one, all
the Northern States abolished slavery, but none of the Southern

States even proposed to do so. Westward expansion and a new invention gave slavery a new importance and a new lease of life. In 1792 Eli Whitney invented a machine for separating the cotton seed from the lint which made the cultivation of cotton much more profitable, and the planters, spreading west, carried its cultivation into the black belt—a narrow strip of fertile soil, most suitable for cotton, stretching from South Carolina to Texas. So the two different orders of society were continued in being.

On the Atlantic coast the boundary between the two orders of society was Mason and Dixon's line—the frontier between Pennsylvania on the one side, and Delaware and Maryland on the other. In the West it followed the Ohio; north of which slavery had been prohibited by agreement in 1787. There was thus a geographical division of the Union on the question of slavery; the North-West became assimilated to the North and the South-West to the South. It happened for some years that settlement proceeded evenly in the two sections, and thus a balance of power was maintained between slave and free States—in 1819 there were eleven of each, and each side thus had twenty-two votes in the Senate. The South looked on this balance as essential to the security of their institution.

The difference between the two parts of the country produced a great political issue when settlers entered the lands west of the Mississippi, the Louisiana Purchase. No decision had been made concerning the expansion of slavery into these parts. The free States did not want slavery carried there; the Southerners saw the opportunity to extend cotton cultivation, and, moreover, wished to preserve the balance of power. In 1819 the Territory of Missouri applied for permission to become a State and so the political battle was joined. Was slavery to be extended further? The conflict was bitter. To the aged Jefferson it sounded the knell of the Union. But in 1820 an agreement was reached, known as the Missouri Compromise. Missouri was admitted as a slave State and Maine as a free State, which preserved the balance between the sections, and slavery was prohibited in the Louisiana Purchase north of the line 36.30. The opponents of slavery were bitterly disappointed, feeling that the slave-owners had gained the advantage. Owing to the climate, slavery was not likely, in any case, to go north of the line fixed. Moreover, another slave State, Arkansas, might soon be created in the area open to slavery, while the settlement of the northern part of the territory seemed remote. It was clear that slavery was not a vanishing institution as they had once hoped, but a living and aggressive power, which was going to spread across the continent and range the two orders of society in permanent antagonism. In the contest, the South had shown its solidity, for while the Northerners divided, some supporting the South, no Southern member voted for the restriction of slavery.

For thirty years after this compromise the question of slavery was kept out of politics, but the antagonism between the sections steadily increased. Under the criticism of the North, Southern opinion hardened in favour of slavery. Whereas Jefferson had denounced the slave trade in the first draft of the Declaration of Independence, and Washington, by his will, had emancipated all his slaves, Calhoun, who led the South after 1830, proclaimed slavery a positive good, declaring it was the only possible relation between the two races, advantageous to the negro and a guarantee of social stability. A new leadership was rising up in the South. The owners of the black belt were becoming men of wealth and they formed a new landed gentry, which displaced the old Virginian aristocracy. Cotton is king and therefore slavery is a blessing: so they argued; and they regarded slavery not as something transitional, but as the permanent basis of their society. Their purpose was more and more concentrated on the preservation of their institution, and to preserve it they felt they must extend it. So in foreign policy they favoured expansion, and expansion southwards into tropical lands where slavery could live. They were partly responsible for the annexation of Texas and for the unscrupulous pressure on Mexico which brought the war of

1846, and they had designs on Cuba. They were angered by the agitation of the question in the North and, when abolitionist literature was circulated in the South and petitions against slavery presented to Congress, they challenged such fundamental rights as the freedom of the mails and the right to petition Congress.

This so-called slave oligarchy of the South was only a small society. Of large planters with more than fifty slaves there were in 1850 about 8000, but, though numerically few, they produced a high proportion of able men who dominated American politics in the thirty years before the Civil War. Half the cotton crop was grown by small farmers with less than ten slaves. On the worn-out soils of the South the small farmers degenerated into 'poor whites'. Lacking education and despising labour, they became the dependents of the great planters, but they stood solidly with them in defence of Southern interests in politics and in war: on the race question the South was united.

As for the negro, slavery did not elevate him, though it is not to be assumed that his life was always wretched. Conditions varied with the occupation and the master. Household slavery was generally mild; plantation slavery, if the owner were an absentee and the overseer in control, generally harsh. The profits from slave labour depended on the system of control. Negroes did not work without punishment and some cruelty was inherent in the system. The freed negro did not fit into the social order and might be more oppressed than the slave.

The South was not a rich country; it showed no signs of the general progress of the North. Slavery confined it to agriculture, and that not very efficient, for slave labour was stupid and unwilling. Manufactures were neglected; there were few towns and trade was managed by the Northerners. Education was backward. Eminent as they were in law and politics, the Southerners could show no counterpart to the many-sided intellectual life of New England. The American spirit of equality and progress could not penetrate the South, nor could the fresh winds of Western democracy.

The average Northerner thought slavery wrong and thought it ought to be abolished; equally he thought it wrong to put pressure on the South, provided the South was loyal to the Constitution and the Union. But he was becoming conscious that slavery was not a dying, but an expanding, institution. He saw slavery abolished in Latin America and in the British colonies, and he felt that his own country was falling behind in the moral progress of the world. Abolitionist societies, though they had not much influence, except in angering the South, kept the subject before him, and the handing back of fugitive slaves was continually exasperating feelings on both sides.

> No slave hunt in our borders—no pirate on our strand!
> No fetters in the Bay State—no slave upon our land!

wrote Whittier in *Massachusetts to Virginia* in 1843, and voiced a sentiment growing in the North.

The Missouri Compromise applied only to the Louisiana Purchase. Between 1845 and 1848 the United States made immense territorial acquisitions—Texas, Oregon, California and New Mexico. Was slavery to spread to the Pacific shore? Southerners did not expect to see slavery in Oregon, but they wanted it in California. The gold discoveries of 1849 brought the matter to a head, for there was a rush of immigrants to California and they asked for admission to the Union as a free State. So again the dividing issue was forced into politics and again there was a bitter struggle. 'There is a higher law than the Constitution', said Seward of New York in the Senate debate, and he spoke for new forces coming into the conflict. Again the Democrats in the North stood by their party, while the Southern Whigs left theirs and voted with the South, and again the old leaders, Clay and Webster, arranged a compromise— California was admitted as a free State, as the settlers wished; no decision was taken concerning New Mexico, and a stringent law for the restoration of fugitive slaves was promised to the South. On this occasion the South felt worsted. The fertile valleys of California were closed to slavery; cotton and tobacco could not be grown on the high lands concerning which no decision was taken—nature decided that. The new Fugitive Slave law did their cause more harm than good; the Northern States prepared to resist it, and traffic on the 'Underground Railroad', along which slaves were smuggled from the South to Canada, increased. So the compromise of 1850 was no settlement; the issue raised remained, both sides pressed their views and the profound difference between the sections was seen to be an unsolved problem at the heart of the national life.

In the stormy decade that followed the Compromise of 1850 and ended in the Civil War, two events stand out—one, an Act of Congress, the Kansas-Nebraska Bill (1854), and the other, the decision of the Supreme Court in the case of the negro, Dred Scott (1857). Both sides were contesting the possession of the West, on which depended the balance of power, and which by successive agreements had hitherto been divided. These two events upset all agreements concerning its division in favour of the extreme Southern view, and thus consolidated opinion in the North against the expansion of slavery.

The Kansas-Nebraska Bill empowered the settlers in these parts of the Louisiana Purchase to form Territorial Governments and to decide for themselves the question of slavery. Stephen Douglas, a popular Western politician, who introduced the Bill, argued that the Compromise of 1850 superseded the Missouri Compromise by introducing the principle of popular sovereignty. Let the people on the spot decide whether they wanted slavery or not, as the Californian immigrants had been allowed to do. It was an ingenious argument, but against common knowledge. No one had so interpreted the decisions of 1850. The Bill started a new train of events. The battle concerning the expansion of slavery was transferred to the Territories. The Southerners, not without violence, established a government recognizing slavery in one of them, Kansas, thus making the first appeal to force. The Whigs had lost their old leaders, Clay and Webster, and the party broke up. Out of the confusion, a new party, the Republican party, emerged in the North, containing all the various groups opposed to the extension of slavery. The Republican party was to become the party of big business, but in its origin it brought together the humanitarian spirit of Jefferson and the material interests championed by the Whigs. The union of North and West against the South was taking shape and the new party, at the election of 1856, came very near to ending the long supremacy of the Democrats.

Dred Scott was a slave whose master took him from Missouri to Illinois, a free State, thence into the North-West, where slavery was excluded by the Missouri Compromise, and back to Missouri. He claimed that his residence on free soil destroyed his master's claim over him. The case came to the Supreme Court. The Supreme Court held that, being a negro, he was not a citizen, and had therefore no standing in the Court, and further that, being a slave, he was the property of his master, and residence in the North-West territory did not emancipate him because Congress could not deprive citizens of their property without due process of law. The Missouri Compromise was thus declared unconstitutional; equally, popular sovereignty offered no solution of the question of slavery in the Territories, for what Congress could not do, a Territorial legislature, owing its existence to Congress, also could not do. Thus slavery, as Calhoun maintained, followed the flag and was legal in all the Western Territories.

Again the Democrats had won, but this time they had won too much. From claiming the equal division of the West, they had passed on to claiming the whole. The Republicans looked round for a new leader and found one in a young Western lawyer, Abraham Lincoln, whom the Kansas-Nebraska Bill had brought from obscurity into politics. His education had been the hard experience of frontier life, but he had thought for himself on national problems and could express his thoughts with wit, logic and courage. In 1858 there was a contest in Illinois for the election of a Senator; Douglas stood for the Democrats, Lincoln for the Republicans. 'I shall have my hands full,' said Douglas, 'he is the strong man of his party... and the best stump-speaker, with his droll ways and dry jokes, in the West.'[1] They held a series of public debates. Lincoln lost the election, but he won the ear of the country. 'A house divided against itself', he said, 'cannot stand....I do not expect the Union to be dissolved....It will become all one thing, or all the other.'[2] Slavery, he declared, 'a moral, a social and a political wrong', affecting the existence of the whole nation. 'Their thinking it right and our thinking it wrong is the precise fact on which depends the whole controversy.' The Republican party would 'so deal with it that in the run of time there may be some promise of an end of it'. These debates laid bare the issue and showed to both sides how profound was the difference between them.

Suddenly the violence that had begun in the West was transferred to the Atlantic coast. In October 1859 John Brown, a Puritan fanatic, who had taken part in the fighting in 'bleeding Kansas', seized the arsenal at Harper's Ferry in Maryland, prepared to force the issue and, as he put it, 'to die for God's eternal truth on the scaffold as in any other way'. This he did and became a symbol of the cause in legend and battle song. The South blamed the North for his action, and, more justly, for the Personal Liberty laws, which many Northern States were passing to nullify the Fugitive Slave Act of 1850. So feelings were inflamed over the whole country as the Presidential election of 1860 drew near. Lincoln was chosen as the Republican candidate, not because he was a great man, which no one suspected, but because he could win the North-West. The Democrats divided, put up two candidates, and Lincoln was elected. Southern tempers, always hot, were now worked up to breaking point. South Carolina promptly declared itself an independent commonwealth and six other Southern States followed its example.

[1] Rhodes, J. F., *History of the United States*, II, 313.
[2] *Speeches and Letters of Abraham Lincoln* (Everyman's Library), p. 69.

The 'irrepressible conflict', as Seward had called it in 1858, was precipitated.

Secession had long been threatened by the Southern States. They realized that they were losing ground in the national life. Once they had been indisputably predominant. For thirty-two out of the first forty years of the Union Virginians had held the Presidential office. The election of Jackson marked a turning point. They saw then that their influence over the Western democracy and the prosperous North was waning. Equality in the Senate they lost after 1850, and owing to the disparity in population between the sections, the House of Representatives was predominantly Northern. With the election of Lincoln all the machinery of the National Government passed out of their control. Economically, too, they knew themselves weaker. While in the North immigrants were pouring in, the railway system was being built up, labour-saving devices were multiplied and industry was diversified, the South remained relatively stagnant. Its young men went West, but their places were not filled from the Old World. Slavery gave to economic life a fixed form and blocked the path of progress. But the South knew no other way of growing cotton and so felt that slavery must be made secure and permanent. They had come to feel themselves a different society, yoked in a common union with the North, but no longer united. Liberty was to be preferred to union, and slavery was the ground on which they chose to fight for freedom. If war came, which they doubted, they believed that they could win it.

Lincoln was elected in November, but did not take office till March. Buchanan, the retiring President, declared secession illegal, but did nothing to prevent it. Congress had no policy and so the North looked on helplessly while the Southern Confederacy was formed. Its constitution was modelled upon the Constitution of the United States. But it guaranteed State rights and slavery, forbade protective legislation and expenditure on internal improvements, disallowed the Spoils Systems and in some ways strengthened the executive against the legislature. The differences illustrated the grievances the Southerners had felt. Thus, when Lincoln entered on office in April 1861, secession was an accomplished fact and a Southern Confederacy was asking for the recognition of the world.

'No State, upon its own mere motion, can lawfully get out of the Union', he said, at his inauguration. 'I shall take care... that the laws of the Union be faithfully executed in all the States....In doing this there needs to be no bloodshed or violence; and there shall be none, unless it be forced upon the national authority.'[1] The South took up the challenge and attacked the U.S. Fort Sumter in South Carolina, and the issue was raised. Would the North assent to the division of the nation; or would they accept war in defence of its unity? It all depended on the President. To Washington, Lincoln was a rough Westerner, with an arresting style of oratory, capable of winning an election; his courage, humanity and strength were unknown.

Lincoln was clear that whatever the cost the Union must be preserved. 'Physically speaking', he had said in his Inaugural Address, 'we cannot separate.'[2] Two States and two orders of society could not co-exist in peace in such close and continuous contact as their geography imposed. And he called on the States to furnish troops. The eight slave States still in the Union refused, and four of them, Virginia, North Carolina, Tennessee, Arkansas, then joined the South; the other four, Delaware, Maryland, Kentucky, Missouri, which were border States, were kept within the Union. Both sides anticipated a short struggle.

Four years of war followed—a duel between the two parts of the country, fought to a finish, with equal courage and persistence and without foreign intervention. Neither side desired war, but the South would not make peace without independence, nor the North without union. To win, the North must conquer the South and bring it back into the Union; the South, to win,

[1] *Speeches and Letters of Abraham Lincoln* (Everyman's Library), pp. 168–9.
[2] *Ibid.*, p. 172.

had to prove itself unconquerable. The North had a population of 19,000,000, the South of 8,000,000 whites and 4,000,000 slaves. The North had the principal manufacturing districts, the great centres of foreign and domestic trade, immense areas of public land, the gold-bearing regions and a superior railway system. Its material weight proved in the end decisive, but only after a prolonged struggle and interminable failures, and only because of an invincible political leadership. Neither side had a trained army at the beginning óf the war, but the South had the ablest officers of the U.S. Army, Robert E. Lee, Johnston and Stonewall Jackson, who proved more than a match for the Northern generals until Lincoln discovered Grant, and who showed how much military skill can do to redress inferiority of resources. The Northern armies took the offensive and tried to surround the Confederacy, to seize the line of the Mississippi and cut the South off from the West, while their fleet blockaded the coast. But their main object was to break through the Southern defences and capture Richmond, the seat of the Southern Government. The Southern defence was offence—to invade the North and threaten Washington, which was near the frontier. Thus the principal scene of warfare was in the neighbourhood of the two capitals. For four years the Southern armies, working on interior lines, held their own in the Eastern area. In the great battles victory was generally on their side. But the blockade intensified the economic inferiority of the South; it could not sell its cotton, nor import the munitions it could not manufacture. Loss of horses crippled transport and lack of boots impaired the marching power of the soldiers. In 1863 the North acquired control of the Mississippi and cut off the far Western States; in 1864, by invasion through Tennessee, they cut the Confederacy in half; in 1865 Richmond fell. Completely hemmed in, and crushed by losses, privations and financial exhaustion, the South surrendered, devastated, depopulated, bankrupt.

Through all the vicissitudes of the war Lincoln's determination to save the Union never wavered. His problem was to inspire the North with the same determination. In 1863, when a national cemetery was dedicated on the battlefield of Gettysburg, he told the country and the world in a few simple sentences what the war was for:

Fourscore and seven years ago our fathers brought forth on this continent a new nation, conceived in liberty....

Now we are engaged in a great civil war testing whether that nation or any nation so conceived can long endure....

It is for us the living to be dedicated here to the unfinished work... that this nation, under God, shall have a new birth of freedom, and that government of the people, by the people, for the people, shall not perish from the earth.[1]

Washington had told Americans that their national existence was bound up with the creation of the Union, Lincoln now told them that free government was bound up with its preservation. The Union was the symbol of democracy. This was the standard he upheld. Slowly his spirit laid hold of the North, confidence in him grew, defeatists lost their influence; he was re-elected President in 1864 and was at the height of his power at the moment of his victory and death.

His policy with regard to slavery was governed by its bearing on the struggle. He would leave slavery, or abolish slavery, or leave slavery in some parts and abolish it in others, he said, whichever course would save the Union. Gradually he became convinced that emancipation must come. In the summer of 1862 he made up his mind. 'It is', he said, 'a military necessity...we must free the slaves or be ourselves subdued.'[2] And he believed with justice that it would influence opinion in Europe. But on Seward's suggestion, he postponed action till after a Northern success, lest it should seem a cry for help, the Government stretching out its hands to Ethiopia. In September 1862 the North repulsed a Southern invasion at the Battle of Antietam and Lincoln felt the moment had come 'to fulfil the promise

[1] *Speeches and Letters*, p. 213.
[2] Rhodes, J. F., *History of the United States*, IV, 69.

I made to myself and my God'.[1] He made the decision and then told his Cabinet. 'I do not wish your advice about the main matter', he said, when he read them the draft Proclamation. As from 1 January 1863 the slaves in the rebel States were declared free. 'An act of justice', so ran the Proclamation, 'warranted by the Constitution upon military necessity.'[2] The President, as Commander-in-Chief, gave freedom to the slaves of the enemy. After his re-election in 1864 he felt strong enough to take a further step and proposed the 13th Amendment to the Constitution which prohibited slavery within the United States. In March 1861 an amendment guaranteeing slavery had passed through Congress, and had the Southern States been willing to make terms then, the 13th Amendment to the Constitution might have been one to guarantee and not to abolish slavery. The Proclamation gave to the North a moral advantage. Henceforward, a Northern victory would not only restore the Union, but establish a humaner order of society, while a Southern victory would break the Union and give new life to a dying institution.

Both North and South were disappointed in the attitude of Europe. The South did not receive the recognition it expected, nor the North the sympathy to which it felt entitled. British ministers made no secret of their belief that the cause of the North was hopeless; and Napoleon III took the opportunity to ignore the Monroe Doctrine and intervene in a Mexican dispute. But the North had many friends in England, and, when it became clear that the war meant the emancipation of the slaves, that the cause of the Union was the cause of liberty, popular opinion shifted to the Northern side. England's refusal to recognize the Southern Confederacy no doubt influenced other Powers to abstain, and without such recognition the South was fighting a losing battle, but Russia, at this time emancipating her serfs, was the only friend the North found in Europe. The mistakes of our Government forfeited the greatest opportunity for

[1] Rhodes, IV, 161.          [2] *Speeches and Letters*, p. 204.

capturing the good will of America which history had so far presented, and the voices of those who were true to English traditions of freedom could not compensate for the coldness of our statesmen and the criticism of our press.

As the Northern armies overran the South, Lincoln started to reanimate the State Governments wherever one-tenth of the population would take the oath of allegiance. 'I hope', he said at his last Cabinet meeting (18 April 1865), 'there will be no persecution, no bloody work now that the war is over...we must extinguish our resentments if we expect harmony and union.' That night he was shot in his box at Ford's theatre by a Southern supporter, and died the next day in the nearby lodging-house to which he had been carried. No greater misfortune could have befallen the South. The indomitable leader in war knew also how to make peace. His swift restoration of the Southern Governments might have spared the South the agony of reconstruction through which it was now to pass. 'Gentle, plain, just and resolute', he had saved the Union and freed the slave; he had achieved all that was achieved by the Civil War. 'Now he belongs to the ages', said Stanton at his deathbed; it was said of a man who ten years before was hardly known outside his own State.

'From fearful trip the victor ship comes in with object won.'

So sang Whitman. The war was won, but to achieve its object the victors had now to bring back the South into the Union, to restore government of the people, by the people, for the people, over the whole country, and to set the negro on the road of freedom. The price of victory had been high. Over 600,000 men had perished, the South was wasted and prostrate, its labour system broken up and its old life destroyed, and an enormous debt had been accumulated by the United States. The great task of reconstruction loomed ahead and the leader was gone.

Lincoln's death opened the door to those who took a different view from his of the problem of reconstruction. The South had surrendered; on what terms were the State Governments to be restored? How were the results of the war to be secured? How was the North to ensure the future loyalty of the Southern States and the freedom of the negro? Vice-President Johnson succeeded Lincoln and, adopting substantially Lincoln's policy, set about restoring the rebel States, provided they would abolish slavery, ratify the 13th Amendment and repudiate the Confederate debt. Only the great planters and slaveholders were excluded from political life. But the mantle of Lincoln had not fallen on his successor and Northern opinion did not support the new President. Many felt that the negroes must not be left at the mercy of their former masters, that there must be more security against another Southern uprising, and Republican party men did not wish to see the Democrats in strength again in national politics. So when Congress reassembled, it took matters out of the President's hands and laid down a new basis of reconstruction. It would not give the Southern States their place in the Union till their loyalty and negro equality were secured by law. By the 14th Amendment of the Constitution, ratified in 1868, Congress guaranteed to the negro civil and political rights and excluded from political life all who had broken the oath of allegiance to the United States.

Neither the Southern people, nor the President, would collaborate with Congress on this basis. The Southern States recognized their defeat and were willing to recognize that slavery was at an end, but they claimed their place in the Union, and they claimed to determine the status of the negro. So began a bitter struggle between Congress and the President on the one hand and between Congress and the South on the other. Congress went into perpetual session, usurped executive powers, rejected the jurisdiction of the Supreme Court and finally impeached the President, who, in a Senate numbering fifty-four, was acquitted by only a single vote. The South was placed under military government, while Congress set about creating a loyal party there by disfranchising secessionists and enfranchising negroes. The 'reconstructed' States were, of course, Republican, and, with their aid, the Republican party won the Presidential election of 1868 and got rid of Johnson. To secure the political rights of the negro a 15th Amendment was passed (1870) which forbade the denial of the vote on account of race, colour or previous condition of servitude. With this amendment Congressional reconstruction was completed. There had been no confiscation of property or proscription of life, but North and South were utterly alienated and the government of the Southern States thrown into confusion. Johnson's incapacity, the misunderstanding of the spirit of the Southern people, and the doctrinaire policy of the abolitionists had combined to produce this unhappy result.

The South was now Republican—a state of things which had never existed before. The Southern Republicans consisted of the negroes, who made the voting strength of the party—some 700,000 had received the vote, though few could read or write—some Northern immigrants, chiefly adventurers, attracted by the political and economic chances in the South, who received the derisory name of 'carpet-baggers', and a few Southern whites, known as 'scallawags', who, to get what they could, or to make the best of a bad job, joined the Republican party. Southern State government had been generally honest and good, but the 'reconstructed' governments, in which the better elements of the population had no place, were, at best, inefficient and extravagant, at worst, corrupt and tyrannical. These were years of misery in the South. Soon the Southern whites organized to overthrow carpet-bag government by whatever means they could. A secret society, the Ku Klux Klan, terrorized the negroes and the whites who directed them. By various means the negroes were prevented from voting. The North, too, began to see that their policy was a failure and after 1874 President Grant refused to send soldiers to guard the negroes at the polling booth. At the same time the Supreme Court by a series of decisions undid much of the work of Congress on the ground that Congress had been trying to guarantee social and not civil rights to the negro. The three Amendments, 13th, 14th and 15th, had given the negroes, successively, freedom, civil rights and the franchise, and Congress had passed various Acts to enforce them, which the Supreme Court now rejected. The Republican party had treated the negro question as one of abstract rights, with little regard to the capacity of the negro and the problem of the relations of the two races. So, after a few years of mastery and indulgence, in which the negroes were the tools of the worst whites, they were deprived, in practice, of the franchise and thrust back to the point where they were at emancipation. By 1877 the failure of the Congressional policy was clear. The carpet-bag governments had fallen and the solid South had reappeared—all ten Southern States were Democratic again. The South had recovered home rule, but gave up the idea of separation. The North had re-established the Union and freed the slave, but it left the status of the negro to the South. New leaders were rising who were not moved by the passions of the great struggle, new issues were coming to the front which did not concern secession or slavery.

# CHAPTER IV

## Industrial Greatness

'As arts and sciences flourish best where their followers work for the approval of brethren of the craft, and not for the sake of money: so business flourishes most where the aim of the business man is not to shine in elegant society, but to be, held in respect by those who are the best judges of his special form of strength. This exclusive devotion to one pursuit involves some loss of life to the individual; but the constructive economic force which it gives to America at this phase of her development is unique.'

A. MARSHALL: *Industry and Trade* (1919)

The Pacific annexations form a watershed of later American history. They brought the slavery question into politics again and started the train of events that led on to the 'irrepressible conflict'. They strengthened the North with a vast area open to settlement and rich in resources. They raised anew the problem of communications between the sections and called for transcontinental routes by land and an interoceanic canal connecting Atlantic and Pacific. The Caribbean area acquired a vital importance to the United States, because the linking of the two oceans was a matter of more concern to her than to anyone else, and she could not see foreign powers established on a route of communications vital to her. American whalers had long taken part in the Antarctic fisheries, American missionaries were in the Sandwich Islands (Hawaii) and U.S. ships had visited other island groups. Pacific trade began to develop. Westward, American hands were not tied by traditions received from Washington or principles proclaimed by Monroe. In 1854 Commodore Perry forced the reluctant Japanese to grant a limited hospitality to American ships. Japan opened her door and came out to look at the world. She became a convert to Western civilization in the respects in which it makes for power. A cloud appeared on America's western horizon no bigger than a man's hand.

But it was with the domestic consequences of her Pacific expansion that the country was first concerned. The slavery question was brought to a head, and there followed secession, civil war and reconstruction, and, overlapping them, the last great phase of Western expansion—the filling up of the trans-Mississippi West—began. So for a generation America was absorbed in her own affairs. During these years the foreign policy of the United States was disinterested, aloof and unadventurous. The aggressive expansion of the years of growth had reached its limits. Outstanding controversies were peacefully settled and foreign commitments carefully avoided. Opportunities of expansion in the West Indies were refused—the United States did not wish to add to her negro population. For a long time her only territorial acquisition was Alaska—bought from Russia in 1867. Here no question of a foreign population was raised, and as most Americans believed that Canada would one day join the United States, the acquisition of Alaska fitted into the American picture of the future. No foreign problems arose to disturb her secure possession of her interests. With the victory of the North, Napoleon III realized that his Mexican adventure was a failure and withdrew French troops from Central America. For some years feeling was strong against Great Britain on the question of the *Alabama* and other Confederate cruisers, equipped in British ports during the Civil War and allowed to escape to sea, until in 1871 she expressed her regret, accepted arbitration on the question and paid substantial damages for her negligence. Everything confirmed America's sense of security and self-completeness and her belief that international differences could be settled by peaceful means. Confident in her strength and in her isolation, she would not involve herself in European problems. The changing balance of power in Europe, the downfall of her ancient ally, France, in 1870, the growth of militarism, the partition of Africa, these things she ignored as though movements on another planet. She was far off and therefore safe, she had enough to engage her interest and was therefore unconcerned. So for thirty years, till the great internal changes of growth and industrial development had reached a fresh stage, she remained an uninterested or disinterested spectator of the foreign scene. The quietness of those years exercised its influence on the mind of the nation. It produced a silent consciousness of strength and an instinctive peacefulness. She regarded Europe's militarism as Europe's folly and Europe's wars as Europe's fault. Isolated by a great ocean on either side, she thought in terms of isolation. She could take as much or as little interest in external happenings as she wished, and in general that interest would be little. So public opinion was universally against an active foreign policy. The mighty population that filled the interior of America grew up ignorant of the problems of Europe and indifferent to them.

But if America turned away from the external world, at home all was energy and change. Another mighty expansion was proceeding. In the years of reconstruction modern America was taking shape. The balance of forces within the Union was turning, and the foundations were laid for an immense development of economic strength. The country passed into a new ferment of growth. Old sectional differences were diminished and new arose. These years were years of tribulation for the South. Its planter aristocracy disappeared, its labour system was broken up, its old life destroyed. But, economically, the North suffered little; its population and its industrial strength grew contiuually, and the Civil War is a great landmark in the economic as well as in the political history of the country. It hastened an industrial revolution that was already on the way. A great development of natural resources followed. The United States discovered that it had the richest deposits of petroleum, iron ore and coal in the world. Out of its energetic population arose new leaders, captains of industry and finance, who organized the efforts of the nation in the exploitation of its natural wealth. Modern inventions put new tools into their enterprising hands. The free movement of men and goods throughout the length and breadth of the land, which the Constitution had guaranteed, favoured a rapid development and the assimilation of conditions of life. The strength of Western civilization—of its union of freedom, organization, utilitarian knowledge and wealth—is nowhere better seen than in the rapidity with which it was now spread across the American continent.

With such opportunities in economic life to attract the ambition of young men, it is not surprising if political life was relatively impoverished of talent. Political leadership, which had been supremely important during the Civil War, now hardly counted. Politics in these years were machine-made. The vastness of the machine of government favoured the growth of professionalism. The ordinary citizen, intent on business, had little time to give to the State. The great parties functioned in the old way, and party organization grew even stronger and was recognized and regulated by State Governments. Elections were fought as fiercely as ever. The Republicans were the party of big business, supporting protection and the gold standard, and they were generally victorious. They had been the loyal party in the great struggle, and that gave them an advantage and so gave an advantage to their economic policy. The Democrats favoured a downward revision of the tariff and expansion of the currency. But the dividing lines between party policies were blurred, the real issues were kept out of politics, and the history of America was not being made at Washington. The Presidents were seldom men of mark. General Grant, who succeeded Johnson in 1868, *omnium consensu capax imperii nisi imperasset*, lost in politics the reputation he had made in war. Political life exhibited a constant deterioration of standard, and the centenary of independence coincided with a revelation of widespread corruption in politics and administration. Power had passed to a moneyed aristocracy who sought to control politics as well as economics.

To some Americans it seemed that in this great period of growth and expansion the nation had exhausted its spiritual effort and was intent only on material progress, that democracy was no longer producing a society capable of moral and intellectual leadership and that American culture was feeble and dependent. Yet all through the period there was a broad advance in science, in law and in the arts, and a widening of the opportunities of education. From Mark Twain, a great prose artist, Europe learned of the Mississippi and of American society in 'the gilded age'; American art and fiction were rising in other centres than New England, criticizing the tendencies of American life and depicting the rich variety of the American scene; and the American architect, influenced by rising land values and cheap structural steel, introduced in the skyscraper a new feature of urban life. But Europe remained the teacher of the arts to America; the springs of original culture flowed but feebly, and the creative energy of the nation was turned in other directions. Business offered the most adventurous careers and the largest rewards; and the leaders of the nation were the leaders in the economic field. To their achievements we must now turn our attention.

Amongst them the railway men may be given pride of place. The railway business was so important to America that it drew to itself for the time the best talent of the country. Moreover, its adventurous and belligerent character demanded an autocratic form of management. From the middle of the century the great undertakers, the railway kings, begin to appear. Some of their names are more familiar than those of Presidents—Vanderbilt, the founder of the New York Central; Harriman, who restored the prosperity of the Union and Southern Pacific; J. J. Hill, who pioneered the Northern Pacific; Jay Gould, who controlled the Gulf lines. Some of them were veritable soldiers of fortune, who rose by their wits and built up an economic dominion and founded dynasties like fifteenth-century tyrants. The first generation perhaps plied a ferry boat on a frontier stream, then had the instinct to see what the railway meant and the industry and talent to start one. The second generation consolidated lines and gained control of the transport of a vast area. The third handled the accumulated wealth. Between them they opened up a region of America and supplied it with facilities for transport and communication, and so enriched a multitude of people.

The work of these men preserved the Union. In early days they had prevented East and West from falling apart, and they repeated this service for the States on the Pacific, binding them with the great transcontinental lines to the interior and to the East. The railway could traverse the barren plains and the Rocky Mountains. The first transcontinental line was completed in 1869, when the Union Pacific, built from Omaha westwards, met the Central Pacific, built in the opposite direction, from Sacramento, eastwards. Three other lines—the Northern Pacific, the Southern Pacific and the Santa Fé—soon followed. Thus the railways, though in general constructed for economic reasons, served the great political purpose of American unity.

To industry they rendered a like service by providing cheap transport between the ore fields and the manufacturing centres. One of the most remarkable developments of American transport is seen in the methods of moving minerals. The iron industry of Pittsburg has been based on cheap freights for ore from the Lake Superior mines. In general we may say that mines and agriculture, owing to their heavy freights, have determined the course of railway building and the other industries have followed the railways.

The railways also helped to speed up the settlement of the West. In the early days the settler followed the streams and the railway followed the settler. But in the 'seventies and 'eighties the railwaymen led the way into new lands beyond the Mississippi; where there were fertile regions they opened a road and the settler followed them. The managers of the big lines were continually throwing out branches into promising areas and thus facilitated the occupation of the wheat lands of the far North-West, the grazing lands of the South-West, the fruit lands of California and the mineral regions of the Rockies. And the great railways built up through routes for Western produce to the Atlantic and Gulf ports—to New York, Baltimore, Charleston and New Orleans—and helped by their rates policy in the growth of great towns as distributing centres in the Middle West— Pittsburg, St Louis, Chicago and Omaha. So industry and trade could move west, and there was no overwhelming concentration of industrial and commercial life on the Atlantic coast. Over a great part of the continent life was thus diversified and population more evenly distributed.

In the 'seventies railway enterprise began to show another aspect beside that of public benefit. The railways became mighty powers that held the fortunes of districts and towns in their hands, and the public began to question the manner in which those powers were used. Always fighters, the railwaymen at first led and fought in the public interest and were regarded as public benefactors and received aid and encouragement and grants in the form of land from State Governments and the National Government. Then they fought each other, but their fratricidal struggles gradually ended in great consolidations. By 1880 all the great systems were in being. As competition declined with consolidation, the public began to feel their power and to demand their regulation. The public asked for low rates and equal rates— fair dealing—and complained of monopoly and discrimination between persons and places. The railways desired a free hand in the control of their business. Consolidation of connecting lines, to establish through routes, had helped the public; consolidation of rival lines, to prevent competition, exposed the public to the dangers of monopoly.

The policy of the country hitherto had been one of generous *laissez faire* to the railways. But experience was showing its dangers, and in the 'seventies began a movement for railway regulation. The movement began in the spring wheat States and was called the Granger movement because the farmers formed little societies called Granges. It is of special interest as the beginning of the struggle against the power of large capital. The Government was called upon to exercise some control over the management of big business in the public interest. It showed the political independence of the West that once again they broke away from the old parties and organized a party of their own to force an issue into national politics. The principle of railway regulation was accepted and many of the States legislated for the purpose. But the States could not deal with interstate traffic, and in 1887 Congress passed the Interstate Commerce Law which forbade unjust charges and discriminations and set up a National Commission to review railway rates. The railways fought against State and national control, and the Supreme Court by its decisions took much of the power out of the legislation, but henceforward there was a national authority which could prevent actual injustices.

An extraordinary expansion of industry followed the Civil War. In 1860 the United States had cotton, woollen, leather and iron industries, but imported many other manufactured articles. The Civil War gave a great stimulus to industry in the North, and the abolition of slavery opened the door to industry in the South. The silk industry grew up behind the tariff. Butter and cheese making became factory industries in the 'sixties, meat packing with the development of the West, and the refining of petroleum as the further West was occupied. American potteries supplied the home market after 1870. Meanwhile, the older industries, particularly iron, expanded rapidly. By 1890 the value of manufactured products exceeded the value of agricultural and by 1900 the city population was double what it had been in 1860. The centre of manufactures was moving West. New England retained its pre-eminence in textiles and machinery, but the heavier industries were moving towards the deposits of coal and iron.

The multiplication and improvement of the railways contributed to this industrial expansion. So also did the unfailing stream of labour that flowed across the Atlantic—an effect as well as a cause; and the vast home demand that existed behind the tariff provided an unrivalled market for standardized products. But the foundation was the immense mineral wealth of the country, exploited with ever-increasing efficiency. The

American employer, with his open-mindedness and administrative capacity, worked out the economy of the big business with a rapidity and a logic unequalled in the Old World. Big business, the massive organization of manufacture, was America's creation. A competitive and progressive spirit prevailed, making for constant improvement. Business drew the best talent of the country. Acquired and not inherited wealth commanded the most general respect. Almost all the great manufacturing concerns in America were founded by men who began life as clerks or office boys.

The high duties that had been imposed during the Civil War were maintained and even increased, and the American system of protection came as an unintended result of that struggle. American industry no longer needed protection and its progress was due to other causes. The tariff diminished the purchasing power of the people and facilitated the growth of the Trusts by giving them command of the home market at their own price. The free-trade South had lost its influence and the protectionists captured the Republican party and were always strongly posted in the Senate, which became the stronghold of powerful interests.

The growing size of manufacturing concerns, which was a marked feature of American industrial development after the Civil War, brought the same sort of problems as the railway consolidations. Combinations grew up that had the complete control of the production of a particular article. Each of the great Trusts owed its origin to exceptional genius on the part of the founder, constructive or strategic. With amazing grasp of principle and detail they worked out new syntheses of industrial processes, enriching themselves and still more the nation. But public opinion was roused against the Trusts. The public wished to prevent monopoly and maintain fair competition. In 1890 the Federal Government passed the Sherman Act, which forbade combinations in restraint of trade, and began its effort to control the great corporations. Immense consolidations continued to be the form of American industrial development, and behind the industrial combinations, the great railways, the Oil, Meat, Steel, Copper, Tobacco, Leather and Sugar Trusts, grew up a still more remarkable form of business concentration, the financial combination. Great banking, investment and insurance corporations were united in the hands of small groups of men, in whose power was the flow of credit on which modern business depends. Great corporations became complete masters of economic life in large areas. Federal control was difficult because corporations are chartered by the States and not by the National Government. Both parties nominally favoured the protection of the public interest against the power of the great railways and Trusts, but neither cared much to grasp the nettle.

The immense rewards of business led to the growth of enormous private fortunes; and a land, once conspicuous for the equal distribution of wealth, began to show the greatest inequalities. Many rich men in America used their wealth with public spirit and generosity. Often they had risen from humble station and represented the American idea of the open opportunity. But great wealth in private hands showed its dangers in the corruption of politics and the menace to the freedom of the press and of education.

More important was the growing cleavage between capital and labour. Throughout the nineteenth century the labourer had a position of advantage in America. In a new country the demand for labour generally exceeds the supply and for long the labourer had before him the alternative of free land. This gave him a standard of comfort higher than he could have enjoyed in Europe; it gave him the hope of advancement and an inclination to move about from place to place and occupation to occupation. These advantages he owed not to organization but to natural conditions. Labour organization only became important as the natural advantages began to disappear, when the free land was exhausted, the great railways were built and the supply of labour equalled or exceeded the demand. The big Trade Unions came into being after the Civil War. Even then the dissatisfied elements in the population were the farmers, complaining of the railways, and the small shopkeepers going down before the great combinations rather than the workers in industry.

But labour organizations remained weaker than in Europe. They tended to lose their ablest men, who were more concerned to rise out of the ranks of labour than to improve its conditions. The mobility of labour and the constant stream of immigrants foreign to each other, and, in the South, the presence of the negro, tended to weaken the Unions. Only on the more isolated Pacific coast, where neither the negro nor the foreign immigrant came in numbers, were the Unions a power.

Labour legislation also was more backward than in Europe. This was due not only to the relatively stronger position of labour, but also to the fact that labour conditions are regulated by the State Governments and not by the Federal Government. The American outlook too is strongly individualistic and unwilling to restrict individual liberty. After 1880, with New England leading, there was some labour legislation by the States.

Problems of national finance were always with the country in its marvellous expansion, and its financial history is hardly less chequered than in the earlier phases of growth. The Civil War left its influence for good and ill on the financial system of the country. To finance the war, the Government incurred an immense debt, inflated the currency with inconvertible paper (the greenbacks, treasury notes), introduced a national banking system and imposed both heavy internal taxation and a high tariff. Prosperity enabled the United States to pay off its debt and to remove the internal taxes. But the high tariff, as we have seen, was maintained, and a struggle for cheap money went on for the rest of the century. The strength of the inflationists varied with economic conditions. Depression came periodically in the West, owing to its rapid growth, the locking up of capital in railways and other enterprises, and the falling prices of agricultural produce. As ever, the need of capital in West and South for development favoured the inflationists, as well as the dislike of Eastern control which runs through all the history of the West. The silver interests tried to fix their depreciating metal in the currency system. But, in the end, all the cheap money movements were defeated. The greenbacks were preserved as part of the currency, but their value was limited and they were made convertible with gold. By 1879 the paper money was on a gold basis again. The silver interests forced the Government into a large use of silver, but they too were finally defeated, and in 1900 the United States definitely adopted the gold standard. Improving conditions in the West and a better banking system gradually weakened inflationist sentiment. The national banks, founded during the war to provide a market for Government bonds and a uniform paper currency, were maintained and improved, and gradually displaced the less satisfactory State banks. Though the United States did not return to the policy of one central national bank, the banking system was brought more under national control.

Immigrants continued to play their part in the great expansion. During the century that followed the Napoleonic wars more than thirty millions of people migrated to the United States—a movement of population unparalleled in history. The stream varied in strength with the economic conditions, flowing more strongly in times of prosperity, when the demand for labour was high, and slackening in times of depression. Until 1880 about 95 per cent of the newcomers were from Northern Europe, from the United Kingdom, Germany and Scandinavia. They spread themselves through the North Atlantic States and out into the West and concentrated in some of the towns—the Irish in New York, Germans in Philadelphia and Norwegians in Milwaukee. On the whole they were fairly assimilable, and though they brought little capital, they brought strength of body and a variety of industrial aptitude, which the business energy of America organized and used in the development of American industry.

In the 'seventies and 'eighties a new stream began to flow from Southern and Eastern Europe—from Italy, Austria-Hungary and

Russia. Railways and steamship companies built up an emigrant traffic from Europe, and the immigrants helped by transmitting money to bring over their friends and relatives. Immigration from Germany and the United Kingdom declined towards the end of the century. The new immigration was less welcome than the old. Various unfavourable developments were attributed to it—the decline in the rate of increase of the native population, industrial crises, depression of wages, and machine-politics. The immense numbers changed the composition of the population over large areas, and their assimilation raised educational and cultural problems of increasing magnitude. While there was reluctance to depart from America's great tradition of the open door, for long a plank of the Democratic platform, free immigration was regarded with more and more doubt and anxiety.

This great influx from many different nations delayed the formation of a distinctive race and culture in America. Time is a factor in that process. The elements in the population have yet to be mingled in one national body. The America of the future is still in the making. But the immigrants did not affect the supremacy of Anglo-Saxon civilization in America. The native American kept the direction of progress, and the mass of immigrants provided the labour force. The Italians went chiefly to the towns, and Germans and Scandinavians to the Middle West, but on the whole the different races were freely distributed and American conditions proved a great denationalizing force. Nationality, so living a force in Europe, seemed to become dormant and innocuous in America; for the immigrants came as individuals, and not as groups, and they came to leave their own national life and not to transplant it.

Dilke, traversing America in 1866, could find nowhere 'the true America'—but Irish New York, Puritan New England, the rowdy South, the rough and swaggering Far West, the cosmopolitan Pacific States. 'It is when the country is left that there rises in the mind an image that soars above all local prejudice— that of the America of the law-abiding, mighty people who are

imposing English institutions on the world.'[1] The unity of spirit
and temper remained. But the amazing growth of the country
obscured the old sectional differences. More and more a uniform
type of life was spread over the whole continental area, and the
problems that arose were common to all parts and not problems
of conflicting types of civilization and different stages of progress.
But in the far West a new sectionalism arose and the life of the
South still displayed special features.

Beyond the Mississippi the cattle kingdom had been established
in the realms the miners had revealed. The farmers followed in a
torrential stream—railways leading and following. Free land
drew them. Irrigation and new methods of cultivation helped
in the dry farming that the conditions required. Barbed wire
took the place of wood (there were no forests) for fencing. The
Indians and the buffaloes dwindled before this great invasion.
Between 1870 and 1890 the far West filled up. In the score of
years the population beyond the Mississippi increased by ten
millions, and a band of States stretched from Atlantic to Pacific.
Thus the generation after the Civil War conquered the great
plains and the mountains. But conditions had changed since the
earlier days of expansion. Then the West exerted its power over
the East and obtained control of national politics. But the trans-
Mississippi West was developed by the great corporations and
passed under the control of these external interests. With the
growth of industry farmers had become less powerful in politics,
and Southern and Western farmers did not unite. The new West
had not the support of the South as the old West had in Jackson's
time. Southern farmers voted Democratic, and Western, Republican; but the big business interests did not divide sectionally.
In the great effort of self-assertion which the far West made in
the elections of 1896 and 1900 it failed; its candidate, William
Jennings Bryan, "the boy orator of the Platte," was not to be a
second Jackson. That struggle, centring on the question of the
gold standard, was a final phase in the rivalry between the two

[1] Dilke, Sir C. W., *Greater Britain* (1869), p. 199.

great economic interests which had appeared at the beginning of American history—the industrial and financial against the agrarian, and the former won. Hamilton had defeated Jefferson. The civilization of the North Atlantic section gave its character to the United States. By 1890 the frontier, with its stimulating contacts with nature, had disappeared, and the greatest and most successful colonization of modern history was complete. It was almost exactly a century since the Continental Congress passed its famous North-West Territorial Ordinance.

In the South the Civil War destroyed a society which might, under wiser leadership, have remained a valuable element in American life. Recovery from the devastation of the war came only slowly. The transition from slave to free labour was difficult. The planter aristocracy had disappeared, many plantations were broken up, and negro farmers became tenants, paying for rent in some cases a share of the crop. The introduction of manufacturing industries began, and by 1880 there were cotton mills in the South. Coal and iron were mined, and these industries helped towards recovery. But not until 1900 did the valuation of property in the South reach the level of 1860.

As regards the negro, the South had won the battle of reconstruction. The negroes have no political power and their social life is separate, but the question has passed out of politics. The South has come round to the Northern view of slavery; the North leaves the South to control the negro's status. In its political life the South remains solidly Democratic, but its influence has declined and it has produced few of the leaders of the nation. Relations with the North improved as the great struggle passed into history; and the old economic differences between North and South diminished as Southern agriculture became more like Northern and Southern industries grew in importance.

# CHAPTER V

## The New World and the Old

'If there is to be in the coming century a great battle of Armageddon—
once more Europe against the Huns—we can no more help taking our part
with the hosts of freedom than we can help educating our children, building
our churches, or maintaining the rights of the individual. There is no
proper and permanent doctrine of foreign policy which does not recognize
the United States as the great leader in all American affairs, and one of
the great leaders in the affairs of all mankind. There is no safe or permanent
doctrine which does not recognize our sisterhood with other nations under
international law.'     ALBERT BUSHNELL HART: *Foundations of American*
*Foreign Policy* (New York, 1901)

At the turn of the century, where did America stand? What
was the road travelled from 1789? What had America meant
to the spirit of man? The weak and friendless republic was now
a world power. It was dominant in the New World and regarded
wherever it chose to speak. It had won a vast country for Western
civilization and given a new freedom to millions of men. Population had grown from four to seventy-six millions. The continent
had been subdued, the agricultural domain enormously extended,
and in industry the United States was pre-eminent. A great work
of economic integration had been done and a mighty nation
bound together in a life more and more uniform. And, with all
her materialist triumph, America had not lost her idealist temper—
her belief in man and her belief in progress. Free education, a
free press and freedom in religion were the American's birthright.
With the liberal assistance of the State, and under the inspiring
influence of great educational leaders, universities and colleges,
of varying standards, had been spread over the country. Nowhere
did education inspire a more confident faith or receive such immense benefactions. The great majority of the population regarded
the American achievement with pride and believed that they lived
under the 'best government on earth'. The rapidity with which

the country had grown involved in most parts the absence of traditional opinion. The character of the people, alert and susceptible, made an electric society, through which ideas passed easily and quickly. For so vast and varied a land America exhibited a marvellous unity of life and feeling.

But some dark shadows lay on this triumphant picture. The natural resources of the country, its soil and forest, had been so vigorously exploited as to be near exhaustion. Industrial progress had produced a growing depressed class and chronic unemployment. American farmers, forced to mortgage their farms, were becoming a tenantry. Enormous wealth had passed into the hands of the few. An aristocracy of the very rich ruled in economic life and exercised a powerful political influence. The press, seeking the common denominator of a vast mixed population, had lowered its standards. Large and intractable problems obstructed the easy progress of democracy. America could look back on a century of astounding progress, but she faced giant tasks to regulate and purify the industrial and democratic civilization she had created.

The problems were caused by the rapidity of growth, particularly of the cities. Economic problems arose out of the power of the great corporations which legislative and judicial processes had failed to restrain, while social and cultural problems were made more difficult by the ceaseless foreign influx, for the most part from the working classes of the Old World. Yet the problems were as nothing compared with the achievement represented in the growth of this mighty democratic State. The great experiment had survived its crucial tests; and social and political democracy was fortified with unrivalled wealth and power.

There was no despair of democracy. Reformers were at work, exposing evils, proposing amendment. American democracy gave signs of resurgence. Once again a powerful progressive movement appeared in politics—to recover for the people the control of its life. It gathered strength from the public demand for the control of the great corporations, from the growing antagonism of capital and labour and from the example of State action in the interests of labour which Germany, the British Dominions and Great Britain had set. The progressives wished to use the agencies of democratic government in State, municipal and national politics, to secure reforms and to make administration more efficient and more honest. And to education American democracy turned, as ever, in duty and hope. In Theodore Roosevelt, Republican President, Progressivism entered the White House when McKinley was assassinated in 1901, and he prepared with zeal to tackle the problems of trust and railway regulation, Civil Service reform and the conservation of natural resources.

Signs of change had also appeared in America's foreign policy. In the early 'nineties she began to rouse herself from her self-absorption. Her economic development was giving her interests outside the New World. Her industrial progress made her a competitor in the export markets of the world. The moving tide of Europe's energy began to touch her interests. She was avowedly not interested in the politics of Europe, but she was not disinterested in the Pacific, where, for the sake of trade, she looked out for harbours and coaling stations, and acquired Pearl Harbour in the Hawaii group in 1875 and Pago Pago in Tutuila (Samoas) in 1878. In the China trade, too, she was interested, and Latin America remained, as ever, a special concern.

It was a changing scene upon which awakening America looked out. There was stir in Europe and Asia. The island groups of the Pacific were falling into foreign hands. Japan had become an expanding power. The Isthmian Canal was a problem. Questions arose in Latin America which revived the Monroe doctrine. In 1895 she intervened vigorously in an Anglo-Venezuelan boundary dispute and carried her point that the matter should be submitted to arbitration. A new note appeared in foreign policy and in the public press.

The awakened interest in external affairs made the recurring trouble in Cuba more provocative in the 'nineties than it had been in the 'seventies. For the moment expansion had become again a popular policy. And expansion against Spain now united, not divided, North and South as in the days of slavery. Cleveland became conscious of 'higher obligations'. The 'splendid little war', as John Hay called the Spanish-American war of 1898, stimulated and united America and touched her with the current imperialism. Spain was driven out of the Caribbean, and America became an imperial power in the East. She found herself in the Philippines and it was not very easy to get out. Rudyard Kipling, then living in Vermont, bade her 'Take up the white man's burden', though American opinion on that was far from unanimous. War in the Pacific showed the strategic importance of the Hawaii Islands and America's long hesitation was ended by their annexation in 1898. By the Peace of Paris Spain withdrew from Cuba, of whose independence the United States became the guardian, and ceded to the United States Puerto Rico in the West Indies, Guam in the Ladrones and the Philippine archipelago. In the Samoas an uncomfortable rivalry was ended by the division of the group in 1900 between Great Britain and the United States. In annexing the Philippines America had given a hostage to fortune and was putting herself in the path of Japan. Equally was she doing so, though less effectively, in China. When the other powers (1895–1900) were seizing concessions and spheres of influence, America proclaimed the policy of the 'open door', and of the integrity of China—a policy which drew her nearer to England and farther from Japan.

Expansion into the Pacific changed the position of the United States. She now looked towards Asia as well as Europe, and in the Pacific her interests and responsibilities must be backed by power. On the Atlantic side the British Navy served the ends of American as well as British policy and secured South and Central America from European intrusion. But in the East her former pupil and protégé had become a powerful rival and possible enemy. On this side naval protection became a growingly urgent problem. It followed that the question of an Isthmian

Canal now concerned her more closely. She must link the two oceans. By the Clayton-Bulwer treaty of 1850 Great Britain and the United States had agreed that neither would acquire exclusive control of any Isthmian Canal. At that time the United States was satisfied for the future Canal to be an international highway, built by private enterprise. The course of events and the growth of her Pacific interests changed her view. She saw the Suez Canal fall under English control and then a French Company attempt a Panama route (1878–89). She could not see the link between the two oceans pass into foreign hands. Great Britain recognized America's paramount interest in the matter and by the Hay-Pauncefote treaty of 1901 agreed that the Canal should be constructed under the auspices of the United States Government on the understanding that it should be neutralized in the same way substantially as the Suez Canal. Theodore Roosevelt, then President, promptly took the matter in hand, acquired the territory from Panama—a state which indeed he helped into being to facilitate his plans—and constructed the Canal, which was opened in 1914. An American Canal had become the only solution acceptable to the United States, and Roosevelt believed that its immediate construction was 'imperative, not only for civil but for military reasons'.[1]

The situation of the United States on the Atlantic and Pacific, coupled with her immense material strength, made her a world power. But strong tradition held her back from exerting the influence to which her strength and position entitled her. Secured by a great ocean on either side, the people still thought in terms of isolation. In the sense of desiring a voice in and responsibilities in all the important problems of world politics, no nation can less have wished the status of world power. She still thought it possible to keep the New World out of the balances of the Old, and her policy oscillated as her interests, her apprehensions, her traditions, her responsibilities, pulled her forward and back. But the arts she had done so much to perfect were bringing the world

[1] Roosevelt, Theodore, *An Autobiography*, p. 565.

to her door. Entering the circle of great powers, she was affected
by their policy. The figures of powerful nations advanced towards her through the mists of isolation.

With Great Britain her relations had become more friendly.
America had accepted Canada's adherence to the British Empire,
and Canada had become rather a bond between them than a cause
of difference. The undefended frontier was the sign and pledge
of their mutual confidence. After the Anglo-Venezuelan incident,
Great Britain was more careful of American interests and suscepti-
bilities. The sharpness of that dispute awoke in both nations the
sense of its folly. In China they saw eye to eye, for both desired
its territorial integrity and the 'open door'. The harmony of
their policy in the Far East facilitated agreements in Caribbean
matters. While the Progressives were in power, Anglo-American
understanding became a political force. Beyond disagreements
and differences rose to view the larger field of human interest
in which their aims and hopes were alike. But the British Empire
was concerned in most matters, and the United States wished
to keep out of most matters.

Roosevelt, however, carried his country into world politics,
mediated successfully between Russia and Japan (1905), partici-
pated in the Algeciras Conference (1906) and interpreted the
Monroe Doctrine as giving the United States 'an international
police power' in the New World. And to impress the American
people and exhibit America's naval power he sent a battle fleet
on a cruise round the world (1907)—'in my own judgment the
most important service that I rendered to peace'.[1]

At home Roosevelt saw his task as 'making an old party progressive'. His efforts to awaken the country to the need of con-
serving its natural resources—its minerals and soil, its forests and
water—so long regarded as inexhaustible and now seen to be
shrinking, won general support. A National Conservation Com-
mittee and State Conservation Committees were appointed and
an inventory of natural resources made and published in 1909.

[1] Roosevelt, p. 592.

In dealing with industry, his policy was 'the big stick and the square deal'. A Department of Commerce and a Bureau of Corporations to investigate the operations of the Trusts were established in 1903. The Bureau provided the material on which prosecutions could be based; and several of the largest Trusts were successfully prosecuted. But the process of consolidation could not be checked, though his determination to enforce the law against great combinations had some result in restraining the unfair use of their power. Nor did he fail to impress the public with his sincere desire to protect the wage-earner and to secure social and industrial justice. 'The labor problem', he wrote, 'is a human and a moral as well as an economic problem.... The wage-worker should not only receive fair treatment; he should give fair treatment.... When I say "square deal", I mean a square deal to everyone.'[1]. Thus he stimulated new measures of social reform on a moral and practical rather than a theoretical basis. But if his thinking was not profound, his courage and energy were great, and his activity in domestic and foreign policy made the President a power again in American politics. To Europe he was a portent.

But American opinion did not follow their energetic President in all this. The growing danger in Europe made many apprehensive that the United States would be drawn from its traditional path into a European war. If those before cried forward, those behind cried back. His successor, William H. Taft, began to draw back both from the progressive policies at home and the assertion of American influence abroad. Unlike Roosevelt, he left the initiative to Congress leaders, and the Old Guard of Republicanism recovered control. Instead of being reduced, the tariff was raised. The Progressive Republicans were alienated. Abroad, too, Taft was unfortunate. A proposal for reciprocity with Canada failed (1911), and arbitration treaties with Britain and France were rejected in the Senate. Returning to politics in 1910, Roosevelt found his policies abandoned, and, determined

[1] Roosevelt, pp. 519, 526, 531.

to reassert his Progressive ideas, he entered the contest for the Presidency and founded a Progressive party. At the election of 1912 the Republicans were divided. Thus helped, the Democrats were successful, and Woodrow Wilson, not long before a Professor of Princeton University, became President. In the same year a Progressive reform, the election of Senators by direct popular vote, instead of by State legislatures, was carried in the 17th Amendment of the Constitution.

Wilson was a democrat in the Jeffersonian tradition, and in domestic policy his 'new freedom' was as progressive a programme as Roosevelt's 'square deal'. He set out to 'purify and humanize every process of our common life' and raised again 'the standard we so proudly set up at the beginning and have always carried in our hearts'. In the time that he had before the course of foreign affairs drew him into the World War, he lowered the tariff, created a new national banking system on regional lines (Federal Reserve Act, 1913) and renewed the attack on Trusts and monopolies. In foreign affairs he continued the withdrawal of the United States from the activities which Roosevelt had stimulated. Imperialism had not taken hold of the United States. She did not want responsibility for other nations, but only lands that could be incorporated and made parts of the Union. The Democrats were always anti-imperialist and proposed to grant independence to the Filipinos as soon as stable government could be established. So while trying to discharge her obligations to the islands, America made it her policy to prepare them for independence. In Latin America Wilson sought to allay the apprehensions which the policy of the 'big stick' and 'dollar diplomacy' had aroused.

The outbreak of the European war in 1914 necessarily affected America in her interests and deeply stirred her feelings, and inevitably it raised problems of neutral rights. American friendship with the democracies and dislike of German militarism made it certain that, if she entered the war, it would be on their side, and the course of the war increasingly identified her economic interests with theirs. Taking at last a stand against the German violation of neutral rights, she came into the war in 1917 as the 'disinterested champion of right'. Her increasing part in the war and the menace of her potential strength contributed very greatly to persuade the German High Command in 1918 that victory was impossible and precipitated the German collapse. Meanwhile, Wilson, by his commanding talent, had gained the ear of the nations, which took hope from his utterances and his vision of a better organized world.

The great question that had arisen in international relations was the possibility of the organization of peace. Hitherto the United States had taken the line that the New World was separate from the Old and that it could be kept apart from the problems and disputes of the Old. But the tendency of progress had been to make the world one. Could a power of the strength of the United States and of its expanding interests any longer keep aloof from the affairs of the world? Wilson thought not, and he now sought to bring America out of her traditional isolation to assume the responsibilities of her great power and position by taking part in the organization of permanent peace. Victory had made this possible, but in itself was only the first step.

The situation and history of the United States always inclined her to idealist solutions of the problem of international order. A general conviction of the possibility of universal peace pervaded the nation in the early twentieth century. The United States for long had set an example in the settlement of international disputes by arbitration. It supported the work of the Hague Tribunal and before the World War had negotiated an impressive number of arbitration treaties. Wilson believed in the permanent organization of peace through a League of Nations and planted his conception in the forefront of the Peace of Versailles. The ideal was given form in an institution.

But again the President had gone ahead of the country. The United States hesitated to plunge into international politics. Owing to her historical isolation, she lacked a sense of international responsibility and had no tradition of world policy or world outlook. She thought it her business to construct a democratic society as an example and to keep aloof from international politics. In obedience to an impulse to make the world safe for democracy she had entered the war, sent two million men to Europe and expended an immense sum, and she now felt a perfect right to withdraw from the turmoil and to be repaid her loans. She asked no advantage in return for her sacrifices, but felt she had done enough, and Europe must now do the rest for itself. The old suspicion of European entanglements woke again. All the problems of recovery and doubts of a new path beset her. And the cautious and conciliatory guidance needed was lacking. Wilson, who, on the loftiest plane, had led the aspirations of mankind with unerring instinct, now stumbled amid the politics of his own country. The contest was brought down from the heights. In October 1918 he asked the country to give him a Democratic Congress and it gave him a Republican one. Wilson would not make the concessions necessary for unity, and party politics submerged the mighty issue. After long debates, the Senate rejected the treaty, and at the next election (1920) the nation overwhelmingly supported its action. Thus the United States refused membership of the League of Nations and the failure of Wilson's foreign policy brought the Republicans back to power.

The years that have elapsed since the election of 1920 have witnessed an ebb and flow in American policy at home and abroad and great events which are too near for the historian's view. The sequence of events can be indicated, but their significance and consequences elude the judgment of contemporaries. Nor is it possible yet to estimate the intellectual progress of these years, the contributions of America to science and the new developments in literature, art and architecture. In the twentieth century American scholarship took possession of its English inheritance, and American letters ceased to be provincial and dependent, and in the great fields of scientific discovery America was making signal progress. The spirit of the post-war years quickened these advances.

The great 'boom' which set in in 1922 kept the Republicans in power and strengthened conservative tendencies in domestic policy and their traditional alliance with the great corporations. Abroad they expressed the mood of reaction and disillusionment which followed the rejection of Wilson's foreign policy. 'The League Covenant', said the new President, Warren G. Harding, in his message to Congress in April 1921, 'can have no sanction by us.' The United States had entered the war nominally in defence of neutral rights, but in reality for more ideal objects. From these she now recoiled and thought again in terms of isolation. The instinct of the nation was to withdraw from its commitments abroad. America did not desire the influence she had acquired and would not recognize responsibilities beyond the traditional sphere of her interests, and on these she put a minimizing interpretation. All along the line the retreat has sounded. Though in time she co-operated in the humanitarian activities of the League of Nations, there was never any question of her reversing her decision, and the organization of world peace without the strongest world power went doubtfully forward.

But the mind of the nation was divided. At the critical vote in the Senate only fourteen Senators were against the treaty, twenty-one would ratify it in its original form or with interpretative reservations, the majority of forty-nine would ratify it with reservations safeguarding American principles and interests. Ratification with reservations might best have expressed the mind of the country. The dis-ease showed itself in the lack of harmony on questions of foreign policy between the executive and the Senate—the executive anxious to contribute to the solution of international problems, the Senate determined to maintain the isolationist tradition of the country. The policy of America had become confused and sterile. World problems affected her, but she would take no common part with others in their solution. The executive realized the needs of the situation. America, said

Secretary Hughes, in December 1922, is deeply interested in European problems, both from a humanitarian standpoint and because her credits and markets are involved. 'We cannot dispose of these problems by calling them European, for they are world problems, and we cannot escape the injurious consequences of a failure to settle them.' But there was no longer a public opinion to support a coherent policy in world affairs. Even on the question of the Permanent Court of International Justice, though Harding recommended to the Senate in February 1923 that the United States should adhere to the Court, its assent was not given until 1926, and then with reservations. Yet this means of settling international disputes had always had American approval. But all international action was now suspect. Party politics had confused opinion on international issues.

So America relapsed to her own affairs and tried to persuade herself that the course of world events need not affect her. At home there were urgent questions—recovery after the war, agricultural trouble in the West, where the combine and the tractor had revolutionized rural life and the small farmer could no longer compete with the large, scandals in connection with oil leases in Wyoming and California, which showed that the conservation policy of Roosevelt and Wilson had been abandoned, and the administration of the Volstead Act. That great experiment in social reform was not producing satisfactory results.

In 1919 the 18th Amendment of the Constitution prohibiting the manufacture and sale of intoxicating liquors had been ratified, and in 1920 the Volstead Act was passed providing the machinery to give it effect. But opposition had sprung into being and was strengthened by the individualistic tradition of America and the political influence of the liquor trade. The federal form of American government added to the difficulties of enforcing the law. Prohibition was on the Statute book, but had not the will of the American people behind it. A popular nullification of the law embarrassed the Government and prohibition was bringing other evils than those it had suppressed. In time opinion came round to the view that prohibition was unenforceable, and in 1933 the 21st Amendment of the Constitution repealed the 18th and ended a singular episode in the history of social reform.

Harding died in office in 1923 and Vice-President Coolidge succeeded him and at the election of 1924 was nominated as the Republican candidate. As usual, the large issues were kept out of the struggle by the two great parties, but the Progressives nominated a candidate, La Follette. The Democrats carried only the solid South, La Follette only his own State, Wisconsin, and the Republicans again secured a plurality of more than seven millions of the popular vote.

The divided responsibility in foreign policy between President and Senate remained the great factor in the formation of foreign policy. Difficulties had continually arisen since the Presidency of Theodore Roosevelt. The President and the House of Representatives are elected by the people, the Senate by the States and Senators are by usage residents in the States they represent. So the President and the House of Representatives are more dependent upon the populous East than on the South and West, the Senate more upon the South and West than on the East. The West had its attention fixed upon the agricultural problem, the South upon the race question, and these sections could in the Senate baffle the wishes of the industrialized North-Atlantic section.

Harding and Coolidge took the view that America should help to solve economic problems abroad, but that the politics of Europe did not concern the United States. They followed a cautious policy of co-operation with the League of Nations, appointing unofficial observers at international conferences. Relations with Europe, meanwhile, were complicated by the question of war debts. Wilson had laid it down in 1920 that the United States 'cannot consent to connect the reparations question with that of inter-governmental indebtedness'. Public opinion in America demanded that the war debts of the Allied nations to the United States should be paid to the extent of the capacity of the debtors. After some years of delay arrangements for reduced payments were made by separate agreements with the various nations. But creditor and debtor never saw eye to eye. Like the *Alabama* dispute between Britain and the United States from 1865 to 1870, the question perplexed and irritated the relations of the United States with Europe. The economic crisis brought the payments to a standstill and in 1931 Hoover proposed a moratorium, which Congress ratified with the proviso that cancellation or reduction of the debt was not implied.

The victors had intended that peace should be followed by disarmament. But the sense of insecurity in Europe prevented any general movement in this direction. Security was the real problem; armaments would vanish of themselves if Europe felt secure. In a policy of disarmament the United States was very willing to co-operate, and particularly she was anxious to secure a limitation of naval armaments and guarantees for peace in the Pacific. A Conference summoned at Washington in 1921 by President Harding agreed on a limitation of naval armaments. Great Britain accepted parity with the United States, and the principle of a ratio of $5 : 5 : 3 : 1 \cdot 7 : 1 \cdot 7$ respectively was adopted by the five chief naval powers—Great Britain, the United States, Japan, France and Italy. Other conferences followed to give effect to this principle, but the course of events prevented agreement and by 1936 the attempt to secure naval disarmament had failed. Following the action of other powers, the United States then embarked upon a large programme of naval construction.

Meanwhile, in accordance with its traditional support of arbitration in international disputes, the United States, taking advantage of a suggestion by France of an arbitration treaty between the two countries, proposed a multilateral treaty for the outlawry of war, the Pact of Paris or Kellogg Peace Pact of 1928. Sixty-two nations subscribed, and the treaty did what words alone could do towards this end.

In the Far East the Anglo-Japanese alliance of 1902 had recognized and contributed greatly to the rise of Japan, which, by joining in the Great War, strengthened still further its position in the Pacific and increased its pressure on China. America could not enforce her Far Eastern policy without war with Japan, for which public opinion was not prepared. The Washington Conference of 1921 also dealt with Pacific questions, and the parties agreed to maintain the *status quo* in the Pacific and to respect the integrity of China and the policy of the 'open door'. The Anglo-Japanese alliance was allowed to lapse, and America's Far Eastern policy was transformed into a common policy of the powers concerned. Like the Kellogg Peace Pact, the Four Power Treaty and the Nine Power Treaty, which embodied these principles, were only paper guarantees. Ignoring the agreements, Japan, apprehensive of the recovery of China, in 1929 embarked on a policy of military force in Manchuria. The United States refused to recognize the violation of the treaties, but public opinion would not support action in their defence. Japan withdrew from the League of Nations (1932) and her policy became dominated by military ambitions.

Latin America has in some ways closer ties with Europe than with the United States. But the United States and Great Britain were the shield of its independence, and the United States, by its Monroe Doctrine, declared its intention to protect that independence. The Latin American States, though glad of that protection, are suspicious of any policy savouring of intervention or control, and have never taken kindly to the Monroe Doctrine. Theodore Roosevelt had brandished the big stick, and Taft was accused of 'dollar diplomacy'. In the face of great difficulties, Wilson sought to introduce a new spirit and to cultivate the friendship and confidence of the Latin American States, and the Republicans followed in the same line. The Monroe Doctrine was progressively interpreted in a manner to allay their apprehensions and to make its objects the joint concern of all the American nations.

A great departure from traditional policy was now definitely made in the matter of free immigration. The regulation of immigration began in 1882 from a desire to check the influx of Chinese and Japanese on the Pacific coast, and it raised at once problems with Japan. This was a special question. But in 1917 the larger problem was raised, and a literacy test was imposed on all immigrants, to be followed in 1921 by definite restriction on the principle of a quota assigned to the different nations. In 1929 the total number of immigrants was cut down to 150,000 a year, apportioned among the various European countries according to the national origins of the American people in 1920. The resources of the country had come under development and to maintain the standards of American labour, the 'general invitation to the people of the World' was at last withdrawn.

Economic conditions in the United States had changed. Its policy towards immigrants showed a sense that the country had filled up and was seeking an equilibrium and a fusion of the elements of the population. From a rural country the United States had become urban, by 1920 predominantly urban, and already it was importing food. While its great industries rested primarily on a home market of immense consumption and uniform taste, its foreign trade had enormously increased—from four billion dollars in 1913 to nine billion in 1925. The exports of the motor, steel, electric and cinema industries grew continuously. Formerly a debtor, the United States had become a creditor nation and spread its economic interests widely over the world. In the economic and financial sphere it had attained a paramount position. Its growing foreign trade and its external investments gave it a new interest in financial stability abroad. The state of the world did not promise stability.

At the election of 1928 the Republicans were again victorious. The problems of national policy, which foreign affairs and, at home, prohibition and social justice, raised, did not enter into the contest. The personal popularity and administrative successes of the Republican candidate, Herbert Hoover, stood him in good stead and he gained an immense majority over his opponent, the Governor of New York State, Alfred E. Smith, who, as a Roman Catholic and a 'wet', was unacceptable to many even in the South. The phalanx of the 'solid South' was for the first time broken, and the Republicans won an unprecedented victory, forty out of forty-eight States. So great a defeat raised doubts as to the future of the Democratic party.

Hoover came into power with great personal prestige and the Republicans as the prosperity party. At the moment, 1929, America seemed to have reached the greatest industrial prosperity in its history—a consummation confirming the rightness of American individualism and American isolation. But the new President's triumphant association with prosperity was destined to be brief. The great 'boom' passed into the great depression. In 1930 the troubles of Europe spread to the United States and there was growing unemployment. Elected to preside over an economic millennium and the heyday of American individualism, Hoover was speedily plunged into the relief of far-spreading economic distress. Normal unemployment in the United States had been from one to two millions. Rapidly the numbers increased, till in 1932 they had reached eight millions. The emergency compelled a change of attitude to social problems: the principle that society has a responsibility to the unemployed was perforce accepted and the Government began to organize relief.

Similarly it was an unmistakable sign that the economic isolation and self-sufficiency of the United States was passing. Immense as was the home market of the United States, she now needed the foreign market too. She must sell abroad and she must import, and her tariff was an obstacle. In his Inaugural Address Hoover had said: 'Our own progress, prosperity and peace are intertwined with the progress, prosperity and peace of all humanity.' The spreading trouble made it clear that the United States was concerned in the economic development of the world as a whole and that for her own sake she must become more co-operative in spirit.

If economic isolation went, was not political isolation threatened? Were the economic and political traditions of a nation of farmers valid for the greatest industrial state of the modern world? Could a state be economically a world power and politically isolated? The course of events was revealing the changed position of America, and new forces washed at the foundations of historic traditions. More and more the executive became conscious of the changing situation, but the Constitution did not allow it to give effect to a new policy until the nation was converted and the powerful and susceptible public opinion of America gave it support.

The economic trouble brought the Republican supremacy to an end. The social and economic order of the country had been shown to be more vulnerable than Americans had realized. The prosperity party could not hope to retain power when in the course of four years prices had fallen by something like 50 per cent and over twelve million people had become unemployed. At the election of 1932 the Democratic candidate, Franklin Roosevelt, a distant connection of Theodore Roosevelt, who had served in the Navy Department under President Wilson and been Governor of New York State, won an outstanding victory, carrying every State but six. He offered the country a 'New Deal', a bold and comprehensive programme of recovery, relief and reform. The emergency, he held, called for emergency measures, 'for action and action now', and he asked Congress for 'broad executive power to wage a war against the emergency as great as the power that would be given me if we were in fact invaded by a foreign foe'. Once again in a crisis American democracy found a powerful leader. Steps were taken to ease the monetary situation, to organize public works, to relieve debtors, to regulate industrial relations and to help the farmers. Within a short time a far-reaching programme of social and economic legislation had been carried through, extending the control of Government in economic relations and designed to improve conditions for the ordinary man. These measures carried further the attempts made earlier to secure governmental control in industry, gave national scope to reforms already made in the more progressive States in the interests of labour, and assimilated American policy in social legislation to the policy of the industrial States of Northern Europe.

Traditionally the United States had held aloof from State action in social and economic questions, and the progressive movement inaugurated by Theodore Roosevelt and Wilson had been checked by the Great War and not taken up by the Republican administrations that followed it. There was much leeway to be made up, and it was difficult to do so many things in so short a time and do them all well. To many Americans, too, the changes seemed revolutionary. The individualism and enterprise of the national character seemed to be threatened and State rights to be disregarded. But Roosevelt's policy and personality had won the majority of the American people and at the election of 1936 he carried every State but two. Recovery had been slowly coming (1935–7). Democracy gained hope when it got weapons to fight with and leadership it trusted. The relief payments, Government spending, business revival, better farm prices and improved conditions of work combined to bring about a change. Much of the legislation had been disallowed by the Supreme Court, and after his re-election Roosevelt determined to bring the Supreme Court into line with the 'New Deal'. Public opinion did not favour drastic measures, but the trouble passed, retirements and changes of mind on the Bench ending the deadlock between law and politics. Roosevelt prepared new plans. But plans for reform and social welfare hung upon the course of external events.

Abroad there seemed little chance of lasting peace. But with Latin America Roosevelt continued to improve relations, inaugurating the good-neighbour policy, and the United States gave up (1934) its treaty right to intervene at its own discretion in Cuba. Only if disorder in a state affected other states could it become their concern, and then it would become 'the joint concern of a whole continent in which we are all neighbours'. The Monroe Doctrine was to be maintained by Pan-American collaboration and not by the United States alone. Thus the later Pan-American Conferences reassured the Latin nations that the object of American policy was to secure arbitration in disputes, closer commercial relations, non-intervention with each other and common action in defence. While the New World drew together, the position in the Pacific became increasingly difficult, but the United States continued there her policy of withdrawal and in 1934 laid her plan for giving the Philippine Islands their independence in due course.

Meanwhile in Europe and the Far East military states were rising on the ruin of democracies. The organizers of peace were outdone by the organizers of violence. America's democratic example was no longer regarded, but her example of declining responsibility all followed who could. The vision of a world made safe for democracy had vanished. The League of Nations, admired or blamed, but incapable of much good or much evil, floated, the symbol of a lost hope, on the turbid ocean of politics. Germany, after the advent of Hitler to power in 1933, rearmed at a prodigious rate, and by a series of aggressive actions showed her intention of appealing to force. Italy attacked Ethiopia in 1935 and entered into alliance with Germany. Both intervened to establish a totalitarian Government in Spain. Japan joined the Axis in 1936 and in 1937 attacked China. All three powers had withdrawn from the League.

A challenge to democracy which could not leave untouched a nation 'dedicated to the proposition that all men are created equal' had been issued. But America felt herself unassailable. She believed she could isolate herself from the rising menace in Europe. Neither her great power, nor a sense of responsibility for international order, nor her external interests, nor the possibility of danger moved her to repeat the experiment of intervention on the world stage. That experiment had not made the world safe for democracy or removed the danger of war, and she preferred to give up the defence of neutral rights rather than run the risk of involvement in a European struggle. Roosevelt's efforts to educate public opinion to the dangers of isolation had little effect. The economic crisis, the loss of war-debts and investments in Europe, the general confusion, distrust of European powers and a fear of war created a public opinion so averse from international action that the Government lacked the strength for an effective policy in Europe or Asia. Neutrality legislation was passed (1935-7) to ensure American isolation in the event of war. The great tradition handed down by Washington and Jefferson assumed that America was free to choose what part she would take in international relations. But modern change has made the world increasingly one in its problems and policy. As Wilson said of keeping out of the war in 1916, 'that depends upon what others do'.

In 1938 Germany annexed Austria and part of Czechoslovakia, and Japan, ignoring the Nine Power Treaty, announced her policy of a new order in East Asia. The next year Germany attacked Poland and war began in Europe. In 1940 France fell, and Japan, seeing South-East Asia at her mercy, occupied Indo-China and waited her moment to join in the widening conflict. The United States awoke to her danger. But majority opinion was still opposed to entering the war. All aid to the democracies short of war was the programme which alone secured that substantial unanimity Roosevelt had asked for. America was not indeed ready for war. But the quickened policy gave birth to the Lease-Lend Bill, empowering the President, notwithstanding any other law (a provision which circumvented the Johnson Act and Neutrality legislation) to transfer materials or facilities to any country whose defence he thought vital to the defence of the United States. This great instrument made the United States an effective participant in the war, with the position of an arsenal for democracy. She would stand behind the democratic nations and, in particular, now regarded Britain as the bulwark of her own defence. Roosevelt, seeking to found his policy on a united nation, brought some eminent Republican leaders into his administration. American troops occupied Iceland and her navy took part in the protection of the Atlantic route, for Lend and Lease implied a safe delivery of the goods. In July 1941 the Atlantic Charter proclaimed the unity of purpose and outlook of Britain and the United States. But, whatever her sympathies, the United States, like other democracies, could not bring herself to the awful step of war on her own action, and the President could not lead a disunited nation into war. In December 1941 Japan, Germany and Italy showed their hand and struck at last at the United States. Their treacherous assault awoke the United States to the mission implicit in its history, the fulfilment of which had become a condition of its own existence. 'We are fighting', said Roosevelt, in his message to Congress in January 1942, 'to cleanse the world of ancient evils, ancient ills.' The United States would defend the inalienable rights of man. Lincoln had proclaimed that meaning in the Declaration of Independence, and America was now brought back to it.[1] No longer could even the strongest power ensure for itself freedom and peace in isolation. There can be no New World apart from the Old World, nor any new world at all that is not the whole world.

[1] 'I have often enquired of myself', said Abraham Lincoln in 1861, 'what great principle or idea it was that kept this Confederacy so long together. It was not the mere matter of separation of the colonies from the motherland, but that sentiment in the Declaration of Independence which gave liberty not alone to the people of this country, but hope to all the world, for all future time. It was that which gave promise that in due time the weights would be lifted from the shoulders of all men, and that all should have an equal chance. This is the sentiment embodied in the Declaration of Independence.' ABRAHAM LINCOLN: *Address in Independence Hall, Philadelphia, 22 February 1861*

# INDEX

Printed in the United States
By Bookmasters